Jonathan Ervin

Foreword by

MY SECRET PLACE

Living with AIDS & Addiction
A Man Who Gave Up Homosexuality for God

LU
Books

A Division of Liberty University Press

My Secret Place
Living with AIDS & Addiction
A Man Who Gave Up Homosexuality for God

Jonathan Ervin & Mitzi Bible

©2009 Jonathan Ervin and Mitzi Bible. All rights reserved.

ISBN: 978-0-9819357-4-4 Paperback

Published by:

LU
Books

LU Books
A Division of Liberty University Press
1971 University Blvd.
Lynchburg, VA 24551
www.LibertyUniversityPress.com

Cover & Interior Design by:
Heather Kirk
www.BrandedForSuccess.com

To my son, Shaun Ervin,

Thank you for being so supportive and allowing me to share my story with so many. I respect the tremendous sacrifice this has been to you personally. Being your Dad has been my life's greatest accomplishment. Raising you has been so much fun, and I have loved making lasting memories with you along the way.

Shaun, I pray this book will be a legacy of God's amazing grace that you have been witness to from a front row seat.

I love you,

Dad

CONTENTS

FOREWORD

J ohn 16:33 states, "These things I have spoken to you, that in Me you may have peace. In the world you will have tribulation; but be of good cheer, I have overcome the world." These words could not be more evident than in the life of Jonathan Ervin. On Aug. 5, 2007, I met with Jonathan in between the two morning services at Thomas Road Baptist Church. During that meeting, Jonathan shared with me the sad news that he had been diagnosed with AIDS.

But, in that meeting, I saw something in him that belied the tragic circumstances that precipitated our meeting. I saw in him an air of confidence, joy and hope. Those were words I wouldn't have expected to use in describing the attitude of someone who is dying of AIDS. But, those are the only words I can use to describe Jonathan's heart.

Each week, I have the opportunity to counsel with many individuals who are desperately hurting, people who have lost the hope and joy that God wants us to experience. In many of those meetings I see the result of sin, which can devastate individuals, marriages, families and even churches. It is not often that I see an individual who has come through that desperation basking in the joy of their salvation. In Jonathan Ervin, not only did I see joy that day in 2007, but I continue to see it each and every day in his life.

This book tells the story of Jonathan's life — a story that has many happy moments but also many sad moments. It chronicles the highs and lows of the human condition. It gives us a glimpse into a life gone astray that is miraculously drawn back to the glory of God's love. And, this glimpse is one that we all need to understand.

For in all of our lives, there are happy moments and sad moments. There are highs and lows. There are times when we go astray. And, we all need to take joy in the fact that God's love is with us every step of the way.

Read this book through the lens of your own lives. You may not be dealing with the difficulties associated with AIDS, but you are dealing with the difficulties of a life that Satan wants to destroy. John 10:10 says, "The thief does not come except to steal, and to kill, and to destroy. I have come that they may have life, and that they may have it more abundantly."

Christ has come to give us life. Jonathan Ervin, while suffering with AIDS, is experiencing life today with more joy and hope than ever before. Not because of his past experiences or accomplishments, but rather because he has grasped onto the promise of John 10:10. Christ came to give Jonathan Ervin abundant life, even in the midst of dying with AIDS.

And He's done the same for you and me. In this world, we will have troubles, but don't worry. Christ has overcome the world and has given us the promise of eternal life with Him.

That, dear friends, is where we find joy ... in the SECRET PLACE with almighty God.

Rev. Jonathan Falwell
Senior pastor, Thomas Road Baptist Church

PREFACE

I had never met a walking miracle until I met Jonathan Ervin.

In March 2008, while working in Promotional Publications at Liberty University — the evangelical college in Lynchburg, Va., founded by the late Dr. Jerry Falwell, former leader of the Moral Majority — I was handed an assignment from the chancellor, Jerry Falwell, Jr., to feature Jonathan in the school's new magazine, the *Liberty Journal*. Jonathan had recently shared his story with thousands of students in a weekly convocation in the school's basketball arena. He had also spoken a few months earlier at the adjoining Thomas Road Baptist Church, where Jonathan Falwell — the other son of visionary Dr. Jerry Falwell — was now senior pastor. His testimony so inspired both Falwell brothers and many others within the ministry that it began to beg for attention from an even larger audience. More than 300,000 copies of the *Liberty Journal* were distributed all over the country that spring and soon Jonathan was taking trips out of state to speak at churches, filming for TV and documentary interviews and — eventually — was sitting down with me to write this book.

I first met Jonathan Ervin in the church lobby that March day. I saw him walk briskly through the large front glass doors, push his stylish sunglasses onto the top of a head flowing with dark, wind-blown hair, and take a few quick looks around. When he spotted me, he smiled. He thrust his hand out immediately and in reaching to shake it, I dropped my cell phone and he quickly bent down to pick it up for me. We greeted each other and he then suggested we find a quiet spot to talk in the church's chapel. Walking down the long, sunny corridor to the chapel, I admit that it was hard for me to keep up with this energetic man. But it wasn't just that he walked fast — he walked excitedly. There was an obvious spring to each step, and I could only think to myself that this man certainly can't be dying of AIDS.

This is where *my* story of Jonathan Ervin starts, but *his* story begins much earlier.

I have chosen to write *My Secret Place* for Jonathan, to tell his story of a broken soul, of that dark and secret place that tempts so many, and of the freedom and forgiveness that can only come from an unwavering faith in a loving, merciful God.

It didn't take me long to find out that Jonathan is a great storyteller, and he definitely had some stories to tell. That's why much of this book is in his own words. As a journalist, I have conducted many interviews in my career and could write on a variety of subjects, but with this one I knew all the expertise in the world wouldn't put me in Jonathan's shoes enough to tell his story. He was living a life with AIDS, I was only observing it.

As I watched Jonathan share his testimony in simple, sincere words and heard him sing with a powerful, obviously God-given talent, I couldn't help but feel humbled by the opportunity to get to know this brother in Christ and be a part of telling his amazing story.

It is Jonathan's hope and prayer that this book lands in the hands of someone who needs the freedom from homosexuality (or any sin or addiction) that he has experienced — even if they are at the end of their life, as Jonathan was while we were writing this.

A special thanks goes out to all of Jonathan's family and friends for their willingness to open up and share their thoughts and experiences. This book is Jonathan's way of continuing to give his testimony long after a failed immune system has shut down his body and he has gone on to be with the Father in heaven to receive ultimate healing. For me, it is a way of keeping a promise to a friend who made a special promise to me the first time we met.

Thank you, Jonathan, for your inspiration in the midst of a tragedy-laden world and for helping others to see God's loving hand in all of it.

Mitzi Bible

CHAPTER 1
A Call To Go Public

When Jonathan Falwell, senior pastor of Thomas Road Baptist Church in Lynchburg, Va., received an e-mail from Jonathan Ervin, a former church member, asking to speak with him in private, Falwell responded, agreeing to meet him that coming Sunday after the early morning service. Jonathan Ervin sat down with Pastor Falwell, son of the late Dr. Jerry Falwell, and told him about a "secret place" he had been hiding in for years.

That was in August 2007. Three months later, his secret was being revealed to more than 2,000 people at a Sunday night church service — a service unlike any other for that congregation ... and for Jonathan Ervin, too. A man who had been in hiding for much of his adult life was raising the flag of surrender before God and man, and it was time for him to claim victory over the battles he had allowed to brutally beat him down for several years.

***

Pastor Falwell, who had stepped into his father's hard-to-fill shoes as senior pastor of the 17,000-member congregation on Liberty Mountain just a few months earlier, said he couldn't imagine what Jonathan Ervin would want to talk to him about. Jonathan, a 45-year-old graduate of Liberty University who once was an active member at the church, had only just recently been attending. Pastor Falwell recalls: "I just knew he'd been away from our church for 15-20 years and all of a sudden I start seeing his face out there. ... I had no idea what the whole situation was. I knew him from college, but I didn't know any of his story — none of it."

In just a few minutes, though, the pastor knew plenty about Jonathan Ervin, the preacher's kid from Memphis, Tenn.

Walking through the backstage area of the sanctuary the day of their meeting, Jonathan Ervin felt a bit intimidated. He was ushered into a back corridor where some church leaders were sitting on a sofa. "I felt like they were looking at me and wondering why I was back there," Jonathan recalls.

Then Pastor Falwell walked through the door and led him into a small, private room. Decorated with an antique table and two old chairs, the room appeared comfortable. But Jonathan was far from comfortable. The pastor asked him to have a seat and Jonathan did, immediately telling him he was so nervous. With a contagious, warm smile, the pastor looked at him and said, "Don't be nervous, just share with me what's on your heart."

Jonathan started to speak, his voice shaking as his eyes began to fill with tears. "I felt an overwhelming presence of the Holy Spirit in that small room," he recalls. Jonathan shook off the nervousness and decided not to take this step slowly. He started off running: "I told him I had gotten away from God, that I had been involved in a secret homosexual lifestyle. I told him about the conviction I had been feeling for the past two years and about God asking me to go public with my testimony to inspire others to stay committed to Christ ... all the way to the finish line."

Then he told him there wasn't much time left, that he had been diagnosed with full-blown AIDS. "And with that statement, his countenance immediately changed to compassion," Jonathan said about the pastor.

Years of heartache and brokenness, sprinkled in with times of extreme conviction, were spilling out of Jonathan's mouth. The pastor recalls how straightforward — and bold — the confession was, and that he sensed sincerity in his voice.

"He (Jonathan) told me that the sermons he heard in the last couple of weeks had spoken to him, 'in ways I cannot even begin to tell you,'" Jonathan Falwell said. "And he said he had committed to use the story of his life, and the mistakes that he's made and 'the price that I'm paying and WILL pay for this to affect the lives of others.' And he asked me if I'd be willing to help him do that."

Up until this meeting, Jonathan Ervin had only told a few close friends about his secret lifestyle and, more recently, of his AIDS diagnosis. Going from a small, cozy circle of friends to the pastor of one of the largest congregations in the state — not to mention at a place where he had been directly involved in ministry as a college student and former church member — was no small mountain to climb. It took him years to get to this peak, he admitted during an interview a few months later. These were his words:

> "A couple of years ago I felt God asking me to go public. My first thought was, 'Absolutely not, I'm not interested,' and I just pushed it away. Over two years' time, my mind became consumed with it and I just felt like He was tugging at my heart to do this. I would feel that in the morning when I woke up, at night when I went to bed, during my workday. So finally I said, 'OK God, if you're really in this, if you're asking me to go public, you have got to prove it to me.' I knew that if God was in this, that I could ultimately trust Him totally for whatever the outcome would be.
>
> "You know that thing in the Old Testament where they would throw out a fleece before God when they were trying to get an answer? I said, 'OK God, here's my fleece.' I'm going to go to Jonathan [Falwell], share with him that I have felt God asking me to go public with my testimony for the past two years. So God if you are really in this, burn this passion into my pastor's heart like you have mine."

The first words out of the pastor's mouth after his confession caught him by surprise: "You know, a pastor just called to cancel on a Sunday night, maybe God wants you in that spot."

Jonathan describes his own reaction as that same feeling you get in the pit of your stomach when you have a near-miss accident in your car: "A 'swoosh' floods over you. That is what I felt in that moment. It took my breath. I got goose bumps. ... I was like, 'God this is you.'"

It wasn't what he expected from the conservative pastor, the son of the former leader of the Moral Majority. It's not that he expected any condemnation; he just didn't expect to be invited to stand in a pulpit and share his testimony with so many. "In the past, I knew all too well his dad's strong stand against homosexuality, and what an uncharted territory for a church or new pastor to take on," Jonathan said. "To be honest, I thought the odds of God answering my fleece was slim to none."

But he *did* answer — in a big way.

"God confirmed to me in that moment, 'Yes, this is from me, and I am asking you to go public to bring glory back unto myself.'"

After they worked out the details for the service that would be held a couple months later, Falwell called in Charles Billingsley, the church's worship leader, to pray with them. Then they said good-bye and Jonathan walked to his car, where he sat alone and took in all that had just taken place.

"I could not believe what I had just experienced. Why would God want to use me? I'm not worthy, I don't even want to do this," he remembers thinking. "I sensed deep in my spirit a moving of God as He had just confirmed to me without a doubt that He was in this.

"There was a feeling of intense joy as I had taken the first step to obey God in this unique call on my life. From that moment until today, there has been an uncanny calm and peace in the midst of this storm. I have felt the presence of God walking beside me all the way. The blessings poured out for my obedience to God were yet to be revealed."

Everything began to fall into place for Nov. 18, 2007 — the day he would go public with the secret he had kept for so long. Jonathan's testimony would be pre-filmed in a sit-down interview format in the studio of Liberty Broadcasting Network on the Liberty University campus. Billingsley, who had pursued a solo career after a stint with the contemporary Christian group NewSong, would be the host. The six-minute clip opened with Billingsley asking Jonathan about his "dark and painful past," in which Jonathan replies: "Growing up I never had a strong connection with my father and now looking back over my life, I can see that somehow Satan blocked me from feeling my father's love and acceptance of me, and as I grew older, it's almost like he (Satan) whispered in my ear, 'I'll show you how to feel loved and accepted' and that's when I started experimenting with homosexuality."

He shared about that day years earlier in which he found out that he was HIV positive years before, about becoming obsessed with trying to hide that from everyone he knew, and about discovering through more and more tests that the disease was raging war on the cells in his body that were supposed to fend off serious illnesses and keep him healthy. At the time of the interview, he reported he had only 42 of those cells (called CD4 or T cells) left to protect his immune system — a normal person's is 800-1,200 and anything under 200 is considered full-blown AIDS; under 100 is considered the critical, advanced stages of AIDS, he explained.

"There are many people with cells that low that are bedridden, can't even walk, they're weak," a healthy-looking Jonathan said in the interview. "Many cancers can take over your body because you have no immunity to fight. God has been gracious to me and I really feel with all my heart he wants this story told and is keeping me healthy enough to help others who struggle in this secret place."

After the tape was shown that night, Jonathan took the stage and sang what has become his signature song — "After All," written by Eddie Carswell and performed by Babbie Mason. With verses like, "I heard you calling and I felt you knocking, but I moved further from you every day" and "after all was said and done with me, after all my pride and then my fall, I was so amazed to still find you there," Jonathan's strong, powerful voice and his wide smile told a story of redemption and forgiveness.

Another thing was obvious that night as he sang — his God-given musical talent. It was obvious many years before, though, when he travelled the world with a music ministry team in college, and when, as a church member, he went with a friend to prisons and sang before his friend preached. He had also played some musical roles in community theater throughout the years. It's not a talent that has ever gone unnoticed; Jonathan Ervin has been told he has everything it takes to make a great performer.

"He had this incredible voice; he could have run with the best of them," said his friend Lynda Tait Randle, who sang with Jonathan when they attended Liberty together in the 1980s and has enjoyed a successful music career touring with Bill and Gloria Gaither and the Homecoming Friends, earning numerous awards and making many appearances with her brother, Michael Tait of dc Talk fame.

But whenever Randle bumped into Jonathan over the years at a concert or show, she would always ask him why he wasn't singing on the stage and was surprised he hadn't pursued a career in music ministry himself. Then, on a more recent occasion, it made sense to her. "He told me he was living a double lifestyle and God couldn't have used him."

Jonathan said God shut the doors every time he made a step toward a singing career. Now he knows why.

"My whole life I really wanted to sing in Christian music; I wanted to make my living doing that," he said in the taped interview. "And now, looking back, I know that God cannot use an unclean vessel ... you have got to be clean ... and it's been a lot of years in the process for God to really get 100 percent of me."

But that vessel was wiped clean ... and began filling up with God's blessings. One year after he was told he might have six months to live, he was still in amazingly good health and had accepted invitations from churches in Northern Virginia, Alabama, his home church in Memphis, Tenn., Ohio, and at his alma mater, Liberty University. The university's magazine, the "Liberty Journal" did a feature story on him, and it was distributed to 300,000 homes and churches around the country that summer. Once the news got out, Jonathan soon found himself travelling to Pat Robertson's Christian Broadcasting Network in Virginia Beach, Va., to appear on "Living the Life," hosted by the "700-Club" co-host Terry Meeuwsen. He also travelled to North Carolina to be interviewed on "TCT Alive," a Christian satellite TV program broadcast to 180 countries around the globe.

God had opened the doors wide and Jonathan, recognizing the miracle God was doing in his life both spiritually and physically, obediently walked through. "When I get an invitation to sing somewhere now it is a great honor and a privilege to know I am standing totally clean before God to share this story to inspire other people," Jonathan said.

Dr. Harold Willmington, a longtime member of Thomas Road Baptist Church, saw Jonathan's talent early on and often asked him to sing for his staff devotions at the "Old Time Gospel Hour," a television ministry of the late Dr. Jerry Falwell. (Willmington is most known for the popular mail correspondence course he started with Dr. Falwell in the 1970s — Liberty Bible Institute — for which thousands around the country have earned certificates in Bible. He is also the author of the best-seller "Willmington's Guide to the Bible.") Over the years, Willmington has become a confidant to Jonathan, someone he knew would always give him sound biblical advice when he needed it. When Jonathan told him about leaving the homosexual lifestyle, Willmington encouraged him.

"We know God is the God of a second chance," he said, "and I told him we need to pray that God will restore the years that the locust has eaten."

Willmington, like many of Jonathan's friends, also knew that once Jonathan took that step, there could be no turning back. His witness would be hurt forever if he failed to keep his commitment to God to live a life free of homosexuality.

When it came time to take that step, Jonathan also needed to be free from fear. He knew he was risking a lot by going public with his story. He had fully prepared himself for the possibility that he might lose his job and the clientele he had built up over 24 years, and he admits he was scared that he would ultimately lose everything he owned. And he prepared himself for ridicule, too.

But that is far from what happened. After Jonathan left the stage that Sunday night, just days before Thanksgiving, the service went on as planned, with a church leader delivering a short message for the night. Then, just as the service was about to close, Pastor Jonathan Falwell jumped up on the stage. He asked Jonathan Ervin to join him. "We're going to do things a little different right now," the pastor said. With a hand on Jonathan's shoulder, he looked out over the congregation and said: "He doesn't know how much time he has left. It could be months; could be more, could be less ... we don't know what the future holds for Jonathan other than this: that one day he will meet his Savior face to face and the God who is faithful, the God who has promised him that He will deliver him and give him victory, Jonathan will spend eternity with that Savior. And whether it's soon or whether by God's grace it's a very long time, He still is faithful and He has given generously."

He then asked Daniel Henderson, the church's prayer and renewal pastor and the speaker that night, to pray. Henderson put his arm around Jonathan's back and prayed these words: "I think of the words of our pastor for so many years who always said: 'God's man is indestructible until he has finished the task to which God has called him.' The world may say other things about Jonathan, but you say he's God's man. He is beloved, he's accepted, he's the righteousness of God in Christ and he stands before you as he declared in song as your beloved son in whom you are well pleased ... carry this man of God in your grace, let him trust you a day at a time. .... Thank you for this treasure and trophy of grace."

A treasure, a trophy ... certainly not the common images used in the church to describe someone who has lived a secret life of immorality, committing sins Christians have spoken out about more in this century than any other. As court battles were being fought every day in every state to sanctify the institution of marriage as one man and one woman, Jonathan Ervin was fighting a disease that is a consequence of that very sin. But, as Jonathan shared in his written testimony on his web site (jonathanervin.com), "The further I've progressed into this disease, the more I've felt God's love in my life."

After making that decision to meet with Pastor Jonathan Falwell a few months earlier, he writes:

> "God began softening my heart and drawing
> me back into fellowship once again with Him.
> But this time was different; the fellowship became
> much sweeter and precious to me. As I began
> drawing close to God, He began drawing close
> to me. Where I used to feel totally alone in this,
> I began feeling the Father walk beside me. My
> fears began turning into peace and trust. I started
> praying, 'Father, please guide me and reveal to
> me if there is a work you have for me to
> complete.' With this simple little prayer, all of
> heaven began moving things into order, bringing
> things full circle in my life that had to be in place
> before God could really use me."

God *did* use Jonathan — for a season ... a "season of oppor-tunity" as he likes to refer to the period of his life following that memorable Sunday night service. His body was defying the odds daily; the six-month mark came and passed. So did the year mark — and the year-and-a-half. All the time, his CD4 cell count was dropping even lower. So why did he appear healthy? Why was he still able to work full time, in a business where he saw several customers a day and where his coworkers had come down with illnesses and he hadn't? His doctors couldn't explain it, except to say there must be a reason he was still alive ... there must be a reason for this season.

CHAPTER 2
A Walking Miracle

On New Year's Day 2009, Jonathan Ervin wrote these words on his personal Facebook account (an online social networking site):

> *"Jonathan is doing laundry, raking the yard and getting ready to jump back in the saddle after 2 wks off work for the holidays."*

It doesn't sound like an unusual post for a single, middle-aged man with a full-time job. But it is when you know Jonathan was dying of Acquired Immune Deficiency Syndrome — AIDS — and was at a more critical stage in the fatal disease than ever before. His CD4 cells — the cells that fight off deadly infections — numbered a mere 19.

Ready to jump back in the saddle? Certainly not the words of a dying man. His seemingly healthy condition, despite the very low numbers, was leaving many medical professionals scratching their heads and many family and friends thanking God for a miracle.

***

Dr. Robert O. Brennan has been treating HIV/AIDS patients since 1981, when the HIV virus was first identified in the United States. He's seen the disease take many lives. Jonathan's case, he said, is very unusual.

"His CD4 count is one of the lowest that I'm aware of of people with HIV in our clinic — and clearly the lowest of anybody that I know who's been able to function at a level that he's functioning at, as far as doing normal activities," the doctor said in January 2009, when Jonathan's CD4 count stood at 19.

Brennan, who has worked with the nation's top HIV/AIDS clinics and is certified by the Academy of HIV Medicine as a specialist in the care of patients with HIV, said it was not too long ago that tests were even able to detect that low of a count. Regardless, a patient with a count less than 200 is diagnosed with full-blown AIDS, and anyone under 100 is considered in the advanced stages of the disease. And when it gets that low, Brennan said, he will tell patients they have generally six to 12 months to live.

"For somebody who has a CD4 count less than 100, it's usually a pretty short time [before they die]," he said. "So the fact that Jonathan's CD4 count is so low puts him in a very poor prognostic category and you would not expect that he would survive very long because he's so severely immuno-compromised. Now having said that, he's had a low CD4 count for years now and has been able to function and work, go to church and do all the things he's wanted to do — which is very unusual. He's in a very small minority of patients who have such a low CD4 count and who are able to function as normal as he's able to."

And normal really is a far cry from what Brennan's clinic and other similar facilities throughout the world have seen in an AIDS patient at Jonathan's critical stage. As Brennan describes it, "not only do they get infections, but they really sort of become 'end stage,' like a cancer patient is. They lose their appetite, they lose weight, they have what we call 'wasting syndrome' due to HIV. They just look like they've got terminal cancer."

At one clinic visit, Jonathan said the head nurse told him, "I hope you know, my friend, you are truly a walking miracle."

> *Facebook, Jan. 4 (2009): Jonathan is drinking coffee. Just got in from church and the music was so amazing and uplifting. Wow, do I feel AWESOME!!!!!!!!! 1:12 pm*

> *Facebook, Jan. 7 (2009): Jonathan puttin the coffee down and jumping on the new treadmill so I can sweat !!! :). 6:31 am*

"He looks like a picture of health," his 69-year-old father said in February 2009. "He can do more things physically than I can do."

His good friend Linda Nell Cooper, who has known him since they attended college together in the early 1980s, said

Jonathan is "stronger now spiritually, emotionally, psychologically and physically—*physically*—than he was 15 years ago. The strength that he has and the endurance is amazing."

But his dad, Linda, and other family and friends haven't tried to look for the answer in medical journals — they know they won't find it there. They say this season of extraordinary health can only come from one place — the One who made Jonathan and knows his body better than anyone else.

"It's got to be nothing but the Lord," Cooper said.

"We're all amazed and we just give the glory to the Lord," said his mother, Rose Ervin. "We know that's where it comes from, otherwise all the numbers prove that there's no way he should look like he does or be able to do what he's doing."

Even Jonathan's doctors will go so far as to say his faith has been a factor in his prolonged health.

"I think his faith and his spirituality play a big role in this," said Brennan, a Catholic. "I think he feels that God has a role for him to play, and he wants to play that role and he wants to do the best he can. In any part of medicine, as far as diseases go, as well as any part of life, people who have a more positive attitude, people who have a stronger faith clearly seem to do better than those who don't have that."

But what Brennan finds even more incredible about Jonathan's case is that he has continued to reject the option of medication, which has come a long way for HIV/AIDS patients.

"Back in the '80s when HIV was first discovered, we didn't have treatment for it; in the '90s we didn't have very good treatment for it; now we do have good treatment for it," Brennan said in January 2009. "There are several studies that have shown that for people who have HIV that take medicines that are effective, that your life expectancy is the same as somebody who doesn't have HIV. That's how far it's come along."

Jonathan had always been reluctant to try the medications, as he was worried about their side effects. But he did try them at first, when his CD4 count took a dive and a close friend encouraged him to take them. Jonathan recalls this experience of holding on to hope that the meds were working, but eventually not feeling able to live the kind of life he wanted.

> "As we watched my T cells continue to decline, my friend begged me to try the HIV meds to help me. I never from the start wanted to live a life of pills, then experiencing resistance to one class of meds, then finding a new one; I just knew I was not the type to be compliant with such a strict regimen. So, for her I said, 'OK, I will try it.'
>
> "The day the drugs arrived in my mailbox they were discrete and unmarked. I opened the box and looked at these pills. The list of side effects was overwhelming to me. And listed on every bottle as a possible side effect was 'sudden death.' I thought: 'Great, I'm supposed to take something to help me live and death is a possible side effect?!'
>
> "I started the regimen and followed it to a T. With HIV meds you must be completely committed to the regimen. Missing even one dose can make you resistant to that treatment. I tried taking these for three months to work through all the unpleasant side effects until my body could adapt to

*the toxicity. ... It was horrible. I had dreams off
the hook; when I woke and tried to walk, the dizzi-
ness was severe. I literally had to hold onto the
walls to get to the bathroom. The nausea was
intense also. But I pressed on. No one in my work-
place knew about this, so I put on my happy face
and faked it every day even though I felt horrible.*

*"We watched as these drugs helped to reduce
my viral load and my T cells began to rise. We
were so excited to see that, but was all this worth
it to me feeling this bad? Was this quality of life
worth it just to live longer? No, I couldn't do this
any longer. I thought, 'OK, I've tried and given
it a fair shake, but I do not want to feel bad all
the time.' So I made a personal choice not to
treat the HIV with the HIV meds. I knew what
this meant — that my life would be shorter and
this disease would soon destroy my immune
system. I just wanted to feel good again.*

*"So I stopped taking the treatment and
continued to visit my doctor every three months.
Finally I was free from the drugs and felt fantastic again. Life was back to normal ... except my
T cells were falling."*

Jonathan's doctor, though using every chance he had to
persuade him to try them, still honored his personal choice not
to take the medications — even the ones taken "prophylacticly"
(not to help HIV, but rather to prevent him from catching the
illnesses an AIDS patient can easily contract).

Dr. Brennan said this fact sets Jonathan apart from a majority of HIV/AIDS patients: "From my point of view, I think he's unusual because he really should be taking medicine; I don't have that many patients who are in his situation who are not taking medicines; he's hasn't been taking *anything*, for a long time."

But it was a decision Jonathan felt strongly about. "Every visit was so tough because all they wanted to do was push new medications all the time," Jonathan recalls. "It was hard for them to accept I didn't want to be treated. I think I felt like I did not want to be a Guinea pig and have them experiment with every new drug that came down the pike." (Jonathan said he doesn't suggest that all people who are HIV positive reject medications, knowing that the drugs affect people differently and everyone has different thresholds.)

But for Jonathan, after not taking any medication for a couple years, he only became more steadfast against it — even as his count dropped seriously low visit after visit. But when God proved himself true by opening a door for him to go public with his testimony, Jonathan knew he had made the right decision about not taking medication. You see, this way the ONLY explanation that could be given was a supernatural one — medications could not be the reason his body was being sustained. God had to be.

One health worker knew this to be true. Ave Connealy, a clinic coordinator who saw Jonathan regularly, said other patients with his CD4 count [as low as 19], if they are still living, "are just practically wheeled in here, and it's very difficult to get them to stand up." An outspoken Christian, she said she feels Jonathan's health is evidence of God's hands on his life.

"Jonathan's eating healthy, he's walking, talking, he's good looking. I just contribute that to his willingness and his love for the Lord and the Lord being allowed to fill his life with His spirit. I think Jonathan is so full of God's spirit," she said in January 2009.

In this manner, Connealy respected Jonathan's desires to submit to what he felt was God's call in his life.

"I respect that a lot and so much so that I'm not even trying to talk him into taking the medication," she said. "As soon as he says, 'I just can't do it; I want to live my life as pure as possible with nothing to come against that relationship I have with Jesus,' I respect that. If that's what his heart has really desired after — to follow hard after God — who am I to try and talk him into taking medications?"

But one thing Connealy and Brennan do agree on is that Jonathan, just by stepping out publicly and announcing that he has AIDS, has again placed himself in another minority category.

"It is VERY unusual. We have more than 300 patients that we follow in our clinic and Jonathan is one of a handful of patients who are willing to talk in public about their infection," Brennan said.

Even though AIDS research, education, and awareness have come so far in the last two decades, there is still a stigma attached to it, Brennan said.

Connealy also sees this played out every day. "Most patients are very reluctant to step out and let their name be known, or their face even. The fear of being exposed is big for them."

But Jonathan wasn't always in this category. He hid his diagnosis for a long time and vowed to keep the disease a secret every way he could. He had the fear that Connealy spoke about — to the extreme. At first, he would drive more than an hour away to see a doctor. Then, when the drive was taking too much time out of his day and it became more inconvenient for him, a friend convinced him to go to the clinic in town. Even there, he took extra precautions to maintain his privacy.

"I would go in the back way," he recalls. "I never went into the waiting room for fear someone would know me. We had a special arrangement with my doctor and his nurses. They hid me in a room and they called the front desk to tell them 'Jonathan Ervin is here.'"

He also requested his charts be kept separate from everyone else's — and under tight lock and key at all times.

"He was very concerned because he does know so many people and so many people know him that he did not want this to come out," Brennan said.

Connealy said she has seen a complete change in Jonathan from his early visits to the clinic.

"Now he is so free; you can just know the freedom that he expresses and the joy that's in his eyes," she said in January 2009. "He no longer is coming through the back way; he comes through the front door and he sits and chats, and he's talking to everyone around here. He's such a blessing."

Connealy also said in dealing with this virus, in order to see any improvement at all, patients like Jonathan have to make some permanent changes.

"Jonathan is sure a picture of that person who has just totally changed his lifestyle. I am sure he's remaining a pure vessel, meaning he doesn't have a partner. There's no one in his life that's going to cause him to get further and further into this deadly virus that's eating away at the immune system. Because that's what I see every day. People's viruses have been going on and on and eating away at them."

Brennan said he believes going public with the news has only benefited Jonathan.

"I think his willingness to not only be more open about the diagnosis just from the viewpoint of his care, but to be open to the point where he's willing to stand up and say this — as he did in his church and as he does afterwards — it's really pretty remarkable."

In his doctor's eyes, Jonathan is an advocate for early HIV care and prevention, and what he has to say may perhaps be more effective than if it were to come directly from a medical professional. In 2008, he asked Jonathan to accompany him to Randolph College, a small, private college in Lynchburg, Va., to speak at a World AIDS Day event sponsored by the school's Student Global AIDS Campaign.

"Here are college students, who have a different concern about HIV and did not know Jonathan," Brennan said. "He talked about his disease, talked about his experience, all these various levels ... and I think it was well received. He's very articulate, very upfront; he's very honest with what he says and I think it's pretty remarkable he's able to do that."

Brennan said education is key for controlling and combating HIV.

"It's estimated that there are about a million people in the United States with HIV and 25 percent don't know they have it. The idea of going out and talking to people about HIV and encouraging them to be tested is a huge help for us as far as trying to identify people who are infected, who could either be passing the infection on and not knowing it and who would be good candidates for treatment," he said. "And the earlier you treat someone with HIV, the better off they're going to do; if you can catch them before the immune system is weakened, the better the response is, the longer they'll live."

Connealy agrees, but goes even further. Jonathan may not only be saving lives here on earth, she said, but perhaps for an eternity.

"If his life can speak and say to others that they don't have to stay in the lifestyle they are living and there is hope in Christ, then his life is making a difference."

CHAPTER 3
The Secret Place

The first news that anything was wrong with his body hit Jonathan like a brick. It was at a prime time in his life: "My business was doing amazing. I had a new car, bought a new home ... life was great," he remembers. Other than some hereditary eyesight problems, he had never had any serious health issues. As he was hitting middle age, though, and it had been a long time since he had seen a doctor, a close friend encouraged him to make an appointment.

He figured he had been putting it off long enough, so he made the appointment for a routine physical. When no one was looking, he whispered to the doctor if she could do a routine HIV test, "just to rule it out."

"I was home one day on my day off in April of 2000. The phone rang and it was my doctor. It

*sort of took me off guard why she would be calling
me. We chit-chatted for a bit and then she said,
'Jonathan, I'm sorry to inform you that you have
tested positive for the HIV virus.' I completely
went into a denial mode. I said, 'Oh, you've
gotten mine mixed up with someone else's labs,
let's just test again.' She said, 'No Jonathan, I
have personally tested it myself several times and
it is positive.' My doctor said, 'Not only are you
positive, but you only have 462 T cells left.'*

*"I was speechless, my whole body went numb;
I just couldn't register what was happening to me.
I immediately began to think, 'OK, how can I hide
this? I will never tell anyone.'"*

Jonathan was feeling desperation like never before. He had
been hiding something so private, so secret, for most of his life —
and now there was a chance others would find out.

But it wasn't others Jonathan soon learned should be his
primary focus. At the end of that heart-stopping phone call, the
doctor said something Jonathan has never forgotten. "After this
bombshell was dropped on me, the doctor said, 'You know
Jonathan, God knew that this diagnosis would come one day,
even before you were created in your mother's womb.'"

"Those loving words from her have given me comfort many,
many times," Jonathan said. "That statement from her made me
realize that God was with me all the way, and that this diagnosis was no surprise to Him."

Jonathan was soon learning the reality of his deep convictions:
he had a "secret place" for sure, but God was never out of the loop.

***

Throughout his life Jonathan Ervin has "fasted, prayed, screamed, begged" for God to take away desires that, if he acted on them, would be sin.

While some living the homosexual lifestyle say it is natural to act on their desires, Jonathan says he has always felt convicted that God did not approve.

"I knew what the Bible said about it. And it was in such conflict with my spirit — my spirit with God's truth — and I just couldn't accept it. But yet it was there."

And he feels it was there since the beginning.

His story leading up to the part of his life he has come to call *My Secret Place* goes back as far as some of his earliest memories, back to grade school when he felt he was different than other boys his age.

> *"I can remember back as early as second and third grade that I was attracted to the same sex. Of course I didn't know what this was nor did I have a label for it. I can just remember thinking some of my classmates were cute ... and they happened to be boys, not girls. As I got older, I quickly realized that this was different, that I should be attracted to the girls. I knew this was something I could never talk about and this became My Secret Place — a place I would learn to hide my identity even as an adult.*
>
> *"In seventh and eighth grade I remember having a girlfriend. She was someone from my*

church and youth group. *This was the 'normal'
thing to do; we would sit together in church, go to
youth group functions, I even gave her my ID
bracelet, etc. Then she broke up with me and
started going with my brother, Mike. The girls
always loved my brother. He was very masculine,
athletic — and personality plus. Why couldn't I
be like Mike? Why didn't I have any athletic skills?
Being a teenager was confusing enough trying to
find your identity and all I knew to do was hide in
My Secret Place.*

"*This became a tormenting aspect of my life.
I felt so insecure because there was nothing to
define me. I was terribly shy, shunned by all the
jocks and always the last one picked for teams in
P.E. class. There was not an ounce of athletic
ability in me. My self-esteem was so low and those
P.E. classes were brutal for me.*

"*As teenage boys will often do, a buddy took
me to a porn shop. We went into this nasty dark
place and put in quarters to watch a porn film.
This was the first time I'd ever seen anything like
this. And I can remember that I was watching the
male, not the female, in the film. Again, I hid that
in My Secret Place. No one could know I had
watched a porn flick — and especially that I was
excited by looking at the male.*

"*At age 14, I lost my virginity with a girl in
our youth group. It was all part of experimenting
and hormones. We never dated but were just good*

friends. I remember being so curious about what it would be like to be with a male, the same sex. ...

"When I was 17, the summer before my senior year in high school, our family was on a vacation and staying at a condo in Florida. This place was so beautiful and all of us loved the ocean. One day my brother came in and I overheard him telling my dad that when he was walking to the beach past this other condo, some guy started talking to him in a flirtatious way. My dad said, 'Stay away from him, he's probably a homo.' My ears perked up. All these years wondering what would it be like to be with a male ... here's my chance. So I decided to walk by this condo and there was that guy and he began talking to me. None of my family was around nor could see me, and this guy invited me to come inside. I remember feeling so nervous and yet curious. So I went inside his condo and had my first sexual experience with a male. I felt so dirty and ashamed. I ran out to the beach, jumped in the water and began swimming out into the ocean. I was so ashamed and begged God to send a shark to kill me. When nothing happened I finally came back inside to our family's condo, buried this experience deep inside My Secret Place and never spoke of it to anyone.

"I graduated from high school and came to the conservative Liberty Baptist College [now Liberty University] in Lynchburg, Va., to attend college. I quickly made friends in the dorms and, trying to *do the normal thing, started dating a girl. But with me, there was no physical attraction like my best friends had with their girlfriends, but rather more of just having a close friend. I went to all the special events with a date, like late-night roller skating, Valentine and Christmas banquets, etc. I played the part. I worked very hard to hide my Secret Place, all the while trying desperately to get closer to God and be a good Christian. I wanted to be normal just like my best friends, Curt and David. Being at a Christian college, I knew that homosexuality was against the rules and would be grounds for being expelled. So I made sure nothing happened while I was at school.*

"*At 19, I was finishing my sophomore year at Liberty. Because of the school's strict code for hair (for the guys it had to be off the ears and above the collar), I decided I could make a little bit of money if I cut hair in my dorm hall. I had a 'Barber Shop' sign on my door and charged $3 a haircut. It wasn't long before I became quite proficient at it and decided that I wanted to do this professionally.*

"*A close college friend of mine was from New York City and invited me to come home with her during spring break of 1982. I had never been there and when we arrived ... it was like being in a movie. I set up an appointment to interview at Robert Fiance School of Hair Design, located behind Macy's in Manhattan. Riding the subways was like going to an amusement park to me. It was* fantastic, and so huge — everything was massive. I was most fascinated by all the different cultures and languages I heard. The interview went well and I was accepted.

"We went back to finish the semester at Liberty and then headed to NYC. It was so exciting and exhilarating. I felt so free ... out on my own. I rented a room from my friend's mom and after two weeks in the city I landed a job as a sales clerk selling souvenirs at Radio City Music Hall. Classes at Robert Fiance School of Hair Design were very exciting. The school was modern and top-notch; one of the instructors used to be Marilyn Monroe's hairstylist. I felt like I was in the right place for once. My dream was to make it in show business. I wanted to sing so bad. I worked in the evenings at Radio City Music Hall. I sold souvenirs in the lobby and we would all take turns running the elevator for the Rockettes during the show 'Encore.' But in all the excitement of being out on my own, I could feel My Secret Place beckon. I was somewhere where nobody knew me. Nobody would ever know. It would be easier than ever to hide.

"It wasn't long until I wanted to see what a gay bar was like. I took the subway down to Greenwich Village and asked someone where a gay bar was. I was directed to this little bar called Uncle Charlie's. I remember how excited and nervous I was going in there. There was loud *music, huge video screens, and guys just standing around talking. This soon became a place I thought I could be myself in and not have to hide. I can remember seeing pamphlets and posters in the bar talking about 'the new gay cancer, AIDS' and it was encouraging all to use condoms to help stop the spread of this disease. I never really paid much attention to this warning. Besides, I was 19 and invincible. It was during this time I began to live and explore the gay lifestyle.*

"When I had finished cosmetology school, I had no money to live on and my parents called to tell me I could come back to college and if I went just one more semester, I could receive my associate's degree in Religion. I was out of money and had no other options, so I came back and finished at Liberty.

"After college, I stayed in Lynchburg and began cutting hair at a shop in the mall. Because I was known as a Liberty grad, I attended Jerry Falwell's Thomas Road Baptist Church. Everyone knew I was a preacher's kid; I never let anyone at church know I was gay. I had already learned how to hide in My Secret Place ... and that's were I stayed. Any sexual encounters were kept secret."

At this time in Jonathan's life, God was still nearby — as the doctor would tell him in that phone call years later — but He was not close to Jonathan's heart. The enemy was gaining ground and Jonathan was not putting up much of a fight. By this time, his Secret Place could also have been called Satan's Place — for it was there that Jonathan was led to believe that the deep longing he had for unconditional love from a male figure in his life was being met.

"Satan continued to whisper in my ear to walk with him down this path of homosexuality, and that this was the answer, this was the way I could feel the love of another male," Jonathan recalls. "Sadly, this was a counterfeit. I never found that love and companionship I was seeking. Each encounter left me more and more empty."

This sense of emptiness is evident in a poem Jonathan wrote during "a very dark time" in his life:

THE SECRET PLACE

I come from a world of creating optical illusions,
and yet I'm the master of it all.
A world of fashion, a world of beauty,
but in the secret place I fall.

A conqueror by nature am I,
seeking the immediate admiration of all.
Ever perfecting my outward creation,
but in the secret place I fall.

Grabbing the attention of many is my game,
showing love to others is my claim,
but in the secret place I fall.

My soul senses great confusion,

hiding my pain in my world of illusion.

Realizing now my true journey will begin,

O Lord my God, shall my soul ever win.

His soul did win — for a time. He received Jesus Christ as his Savior in 1985, two years after he graduated from Liberty. Although he had grown up in the church and was the son of a preacher, before this he knew he didn't have the desires to know God and live for God like his best friends in college did. He said he started wondering to himself, 'If you're saved, then why don't you have the desires that 'real' Christians have?'" There was a battle going on in his mind — and his heart.

One day in September 1985 he felt it was time to surrender both.

"I was alone in my apartment drinking coffee one morning before going in to work. It was a beautiful day, the sun was beaming in from the sliding glass doors to the balcony, the temperature was perfect … and then all of the sudden I began to sense something in the room with me.

"It was so strange because I knew no one was in my tiny, one-bedroom apartment but me. I looked around and thought, what is going on? This presence got stronger and stronger as if it was filling the living room where I was seated on the sofa. The hair began to raise on the back of my neck as I became aware — God was meeting with me.

His presence was filling that room. I just knew what it was. As it continued to get stronger, I got off my sofa and on my knees. I began to weep. I started thinking to myself, 'Why are you crying?' It wasn't a feeling of fear; I wasn't scared, but I was feeling this amazing love of God for me. God was meeting with me, right where I was ... a sinner in need of a Savior.

"I then buried my face in the fibers of the carpet. I knew without a doubt a Holy God was meeting with me. It was like a search light was turned on inside my heart and the Holy Spirit was drawing me. I then began confessing my sin before the Father, especially the sin of homosexuality.

"I had begged God all through my life to please take away this same-sex attraction and it never happened. But as honest as I could be, I remember praying and saying, 'God, I love you and want to be closer to you. If you will help me with this sin ... I will live for you. The love of God was so overwhelming that I realized my sin was separating me from that — that was the love I wanted. So I began confessing to the Father and just gave this to God. I said, 'Take this part of me, forgive me.' So that started a real turn-around in my life. I surrendered my heart to Christ and asked Him to take my life and help me to live for Him. It was amazing, I felt so cleansed, I felt new ... and now I had a new faith and a strength to live a life that would honor God.

"When a person gives his life to Christ, the Bible teaches that that person becomes a new creature and that old things are passed away, and that all things become new. And that is exactly what happened to me. It has been a long process, but God began a work that day in my heart and life."

Like many 20-somethings who become tired of living alone and long for companionship and the love of family around them once again, Jonathan started to "dream the American dream," as he calls it. He had been dating a woman who had become a best friend. He saw marriage on the horizon. With his new life in God and a desire to know His Savior even more, he proposed and they were married on June 20, 1986.

"Wow, it was happening — the American Dream. I have a wife, a home, and in a couple of months we discovered we were expecting a baby. The joy was intense," he recalls.

Jonny Ervin met Ellen Tomlin through a mutual friend. They joined each other at Liberty Baptist College late-night skates every Friday night.

"I found out that he cut hair so I started going to him," Ellen recalls. "And we just became best friends. He was very friendly, nice, fun to be around. He's very likeable. He's just got that aura about him; he knows how to talk to people, what words to use."

At first, they enjoyed married life. They were faithful in attending church and were even baptized together when she was seven months pregnant.

Jonathan cut hair in a salon off the side of their home and they spent much time together. When they had their son, Ellen was a stay-at-home mom and Jonathan continued to build his clientele. But after a couple years, they began to drift apart.

To everyone on the outside, they looked and acted like a pretty normal family, Ellen said. "I had people tell me afterward, when they knew we were separated, that they never knew there was a problem. There were plenty of problems, but we just never showed it in public."

But the problems weren't about Jonathan's same-sex attraction, which he suppressed and never acted on during the marriage. Their problems were more along the lines of typical incompatibility issues many couples have.

"I was unhappy because I wasn't in love with her," he said. "We were like two good friends sharing a home and a child."

Jonathan said he was "completely faithful" to Ellen during those six-and-a-half years of marriage, and Ellen said she doesn't have any evidence to the contrary.

"We mutually decided it wasn't working out; he didn't leave me for a man," she said. Besides, she always knew his whereabouts. "He worked in the salon and then came in and went to sleep every night. I always knew where he was."

But while Ellen said she had heard rumors about Jonathan before they got married, she refused to believe them and pushed them to the back of her mind. And after their son, Shaun, was born, the focus was always on him and his needs. After the divorce, Jonathan and Ellen committed to co-parent him; he was with his mom during the week and would go to his dad's on the weekend.

Jonathan said even though they had mutually agreed to the divorce, he began to feel ashamed because of it and stopped going to church.

"My sorrow over this broken home became more than I could handle. I had no family here in Lynchburg, they were all 12 hours away. I felt so defeated. I can remember going home to my small duplex apartment, grabbing the big sofa pillow and burying my face in it so I could scream and cry without my next-door neighbor hearing me."

It was in this dark time that the Secret Place began to beckon once again. Like a small leak in a water pipe that is neglected over time, Jonathan's fleshly desires gave way and he was no longer meeting with God in His holy place — the Secret Place was making lots of promises now. He thought it was there that he could patch up his life, cover over his troubles and feel secure once again.

"We all have a weakness in our wall. Even though this was an area God has given me victory in, when I was down, depressed because of the divorce and hurting, that temptation came back [saying], 'Walk with me and I can show you how to feel love, comfort, and all those things again.' ... It was then that I yielded to temptation and reopened the door to my Secret Place.

"The enemy always comes around when we are down and broken. Again, Satan began to whisper in my ear, 'Hey Jonathan, you're not married now, it won't be adultery. Go ahead, find a male friend again, you know how that will make

you feel good and help with all this pain and lone-
liness you are experiencing.' ... And it wasn't long
until again I was living a secret gay life. And now,
more than ever, I had to keep it a secret because I
was a father and I would never want to expose my
child to this side of me."

But again, this secret was no secret to God — His plan
was in motion.

A longtime friend, Robin Bernard, was visiting Jonathan
one day during this dark time in his life. She looked at
him across the room and, for no apparent reason, almost
prophesied out loud: "Jonny Ervin, the day will come when
you will publicly stand and testify how God has led you out of
this lifestyle."

Perhaps God was speaking through Jonathan's friend that
day, but it would still be years before he would begin to see
God's hand in his life.

CHAPTER 4
Out On My Own

During his first year of marriage, in 1986, Jonathan and his wife learned they were expecting. Starting a family was a dream they both shared. As they lay in bed one night, Jonathan recalls being so excited about the news that he couldn't wait to tell his parents back in Memphis. His sister Pam was already expecting the first grandchild in February and his baby would be born later that July.

"I dialed the number and got both my mom and dad on the phone. My wife and I had both ears pressed up to the phone. I said, 'Hey Mom and Dad, how would you guys like to be grandparents again in July?'

There was dead silence on the phone. ... And my dad's first comment was, 'Son, I hope you are financially set for this.'"

It wasn't what Jonathan expected. There was immediate concern where he was hoping to hear shouts of joy. "We got off the phone and I began to sob," he said. "Again, somehow wanting my dad's approval and acceptance … that comment ripped off the scabs of previous wounds in my soul where my dad had hurt my spirit many times before."

The hurt he speaks about was with him for many years, even before that special time in his life when he became a father himself. But when God started restoring Jonathan's soul a few years before he would go public with the news that he had AIDS, He was also at work in the relationship between he and his father that had been strained for so long.

"Sometime in 2004 or 2005 I began having thoughts of going public with my testimony of having AIDS," Jonathan said. "Unbeknownst to me, there was something that had to happen before I could possibly stand before people and tell my story. And that was the deep-seeded bitterness toward my father."

***

Jonathan Christopher Ervin, who went by "Jonny" in his younger years, was born to Jimmy and Rose Ervin on March 4, 1962. He was their third child. When he was about 5 years old, his parents became Christians and Jimmy started studying to be in the ministry. For 15 years, Jimmy was an associate pastor at Broadway Baptist Church in Memphis, Tenn., — one of the fastest growing churches in the state at that time and very successful. "My dad was always working at the church," Jonathan recalls. Later, Jimmy Ervin started the Pro Missions organization and has devoted many years to providing support for missionaries. His wife has worked alongside him all the way.

The Ervin family of six — with the children all one year apart: Pam the oldest, then Mike, then Jonny, and the youngest, Penny — said they were always close-knit.

Jonathan has special memories from his early childhood.

"We had a wonderful home full of love. When we would walk into church, it looked like a family of ducks following behind the parents because we were just one year apart in age.

"When we were very small we lived in a ranch-style house in Jackson, Tenn. My father was studying in seminary to be a preacher. We didn't have a lot of material things, but we never realized it. In our small house, the living room was totally empty except for one piece of furniture and that was the piano my parents bought for Pam to begin taking lessons. The four of us would get in there by ourselves and hold pretend church services. Pam would play the piano, I would lead the music, Mike would take the offering, and Penny would preach. We had so much fun just being with each other.

"Our family vacations always were to wherever the Southern Baptist conventions were held. My parents would pack up the station wagon with the wood grain down the side and off we would go. All us kids would be so excited because we knew we would be going to an amusement park

*and would get to ride the rides. Pam and I always
teamed up together and then Mike and Penny."*

Pam and Jonny relived some of those memories when Jonny
turned 47 on March 4, 2009, as they celebrated at Disney World.

"We were like two little kids again, sharing family vacation.
Pam made this particular birthday more special than ever."

Jonathan remembers holiday celebrations at the Ervin
household were always full of laughter — and magic.

> *"Christmas for the Ervin family was always
> magical to me. The excitement would always build
> from the time Mom would get out the Christmas
> tree and include all of us kids in the decorating.*
>
> *"One Christmas we had snow, which was
> rare. When we woke up my dad called us to the
> front door to look at the snow. He then said,
> 'Look, there's Santa's footprints.' My dad had
> gone out in the snow and then took a broom to
> erase some of his footprints to create the illusion
> Santa had flown away in his sleigh with the rein-
> deer. It was magical to us at that tender age of
> make-believe."*

Jimmy Ervin may have created some "magic" and fun times
for his family, but as Jonny grew older, Jimmy soon learned he
could not work magic on his relationship with his son.

"Day to day our family has always been extremely close,"
said Jimmy Ervin in a 2009 interview. "Our children love each
other, they love us and I don't know that there were any

unhappy times with the kids ... except when Jonny showed some real parts of rebellion."

His mother Rose said she noticed it early on.

"There was always a sense in pulling away or wanting to reject our authority — always — even from an early child, in kindergarten," she said. "There was always that noticeable difference."

Jonny remembers feeling confused at a young age, not knowing how to handle the feelings he had that set him apart from other boys his age. Perhaps that confusion manifested itself in outright rebellion to any authority — especially his father.

"Growing up in a preacher's home, going to a Christian school, a Christian college, you can imagine how that [same-sex attraction] would torment somebody who feels like they're different, and I was asking, 'Where did this come from? How do I deal with this?' I was never introduced to anything of the gay lifestyle. I was never abused in any way. There was never an introduction to this; it was just there. When I say we're all born into a sin nature, maybe that was mine."

But his parents said they never saw any signs that Jonny had these feelings as a youngster. And as Jonny got older and began to understand the feelings and was able to give them a name, he was too embarrassed to talk to his parents about it. After all, those topics were never discussed in his home, he said.

Jimmy and Rose Ervin said they raised all their children the same way, but Jonathan said he felt a distance between his dad that his siblings never felt. And, as was demonstrated years later when he called his parents to tell them they'd be having another grandbaby and was let down by his dad's reaction, he didn't feel his dad's loving concern, but rather that his dad did not accept him.

"Growing up, I always felt like my dad was ashamed of me. I just couldn't be that son that I felt like he wanted. I grew up with great fear of my dad. His temper was fierce with me. Being a preacher, he had a loud, commanding voice.

"And as I was in that rebellious teenager stage, when my dad would raise his voice at me and start shouting and yelling at me, it quickly began to break my spirit. This left such a mark on me that all through my life if a male authority figure ever raised their voice to me, it would shatter me on the inside. It was a reminder of my dad and how I felt when he screamed at me.

"I began to resent and harbor bitterness and unforgiveness in my heart toward my dad. Whenever the family got together for special occasions, you could always feel this undercurrent, a bad vibe between Dad and I. We hardly ever talked or communicated with one another. And when we did, it was very surface chit-chat. I know this was hard on my mom because she could see this deep bitterness I had toward my dad, but this was her husband, the man she loved."

If it was part of a rebellious spirit that brewed in Jonathan's childhood, like his parents have said, it all boiled over when he decided to leave college — against his parents' wishes — and go to New York City to study hairstyling at a cosmetology school and try his hand at show business. "He was totally on his own," his mother said. The Ervins had planned many years earlier for all their children to attend the new Liberty Baptist College (now Liberty University), started by Rev. Jerry Falwell and Dr. Elmer Towns.

"I believed it matched the training we were trying to give them under the Lordship of Christ, the convictions we had, the strong emphasis on the family, on the church, on their own personal holiness ... that our kids would not miss being away from 'home' in regards to the training they would receive ... that they wouldn't miss a beat," Jimmy Ervin said.

His siblings Pam and Mike were attending there with Jonathan when he decided to go out on his own. New York City fascinated him. It was there that he learned a trade that would become a successful career. But that decision at age 19 was also what drew a deeper wedge between him and his dad.

> *"I called my parents and told my dad I wanted to go to cosmetology school and how I had been accepted at this school in New York City. As with many other things in my life, my dad did not agree with me. He said, 'If you want to go to hair school and get your license, you can go to a school there in Lynchburg or you can come home and go to a school in Memphis, but you are not going to NYC.'*
>
> *"My deep rebellion welled up in me and for the first time I felt the strength to stand up to my dad. I told him that I was going anyway. He was quick to anger and his voice raised over the phone and told me that I was disobeying his wishes and that if I went, he would cut me off without a dime*

*and if I wanted to be on my own, 'By God, YOU
WILL BE ON YOUR OWN.' And the conversation ended.*"

Many years later, Jimmy Ervin explains it this way: "There's
never been a time that we haven't loved Jonny unconditionally; sometimes raising children requires what Dr. [James]
Dobson calls 'tough love.' You reach a point sometimes with a
child where you just have to turn him or her over to the Lord;
nothing you say is going to be accepted. A child in rebellion
views everything you say as preaching or unacceptable or viewed
as 'You don't want me to be this, that or the other.' What a
parent has to do in situations like this is just commit him to the
Lord, and that was done."

But at the time, Jonny only heard harsh words and not the
heartbeats of parents who wanted to protect their son from the
bad influences of a secular world.

*"This was heartbreaking to my parents and
they were a nervous wreck for their 19-year-old
son in NYC. This really strained our relationship,
but I was determined to live my life as I wanted it,
not as they had wanted for me.*

*"Now, being a 47-year-old parent myself and
in looking back over my life, I think that even
though my parents thought they were doing the
right thing ... in reality, they dropped me emotionally like a hot potato — as they say, 'turned me
over completely to God.' Ironically they did this
at a time I needed them more than ever in my life.
This was also a tool Satan used to help me fill in*

this empty void I had in my heart, to feel love and
that someone was proud of me."

Jonathan thought he could find that in the bright lights of
New York City. His desire to be on stage was growing daily and
almost overwhelmed him. But a missed opportunity for a role
in a Broadway musical became just another reason for him to
harbor bitterness toward his father and, perhaps, life in general.

"In New York City, while working at Radio City Music Hall,
I saw an open call for a show in the weekly news publication
'Back Stage.' The show, 'Dreamgirls,' was sweeping the nation
and becoming one of the biggest hits on Broadway. I got all the
info and headed to the audition. The show had mostly an all-
black cast, except for one white guy who sang a short song titled
'Cadillac Car.' I went into the theater backstage in the Broadway theater district and there were many people there; there
were only a few white faces. Everyone was singing and warming
up their voices and all the dancers were stretching. I was so
excited about this rare opportunity. Could this be it, could this
be my lucky break into show business? Finally they called my
name: 'Jonny Ervin.' I went out on the stage, and in the house
was one little desk lamp where the producer sat. As we all
listened intently offstage to the others auditioning, many would
only get out a few words and the producer would say, 'Thank
you. Next.' So I sang a Barry Manilow song called 'Daybreak.'
It was lively, upbeat and showcased my range. When I started
singing, the producer didn't cut me off, instead he allowed me
to finish the whole song. He then asked if I happened to know
the song 'Cadillac Car' from the show. I promptly smiled and
said, 'Yes sir.' He sent a piano player up on stage and I started

singing it. When I finished the song, everyone backstage was screaming and applauding me. I couldn't believe it.

"The producer got out my stat sheet and made sure all the info was correct. He said they were putting together a road team that would tour all over the country performing 'Dreamgirls.' I thanked him and he said, 'We'll be in touch.'

"As I walked off stage and into the wings, everyone was smiling, patting me on the back; it was amazing. As I walked out on the street on Broadway my feet were hardly touching the ground. I was overjoyed at this possibility. I remember calling my mom, I was so excited I could hardly speak. I said, 'Mom, you will not believe what has just happened.' I relayed the story to her and there was a brief pause. Then she said, 'Son, we aren't the least bit interested in that, you know how we feel about that music.'

"Growing up my parents did not approve of any 'secular' music; they would only let us listen to Christian music. My elation quickly plummeted to rock bottom. I went into the dressing room and wept uncontrollably. My heart was broken. I couldn't understand why my mom could not be happy for me."

"When I had finished cosmetology school, and had run out of money in NYC, my parents called to tell me I could come back to Liberty. So, having no other options, I did. Not only did I have to leave NYC, but I had to leave my contact with 'Dreamgirls.' I had learned that the producer wanted me to come to callback in the spring."

New York City had not turned out as Jonathan had hoped, his father said. But Jonathan's deepest hurt in all of it was in the relationship with his dad, one he thought at that time was beyond repair.

"I can remember through life whenever I would watch a movie where the content was about a reconciliation between a father and son, it would deeply upset me and I would began to cry deep, sobbing tears. I wanted that from my dad. Why couldn't my dad and I be close?"

Curt Motsinger, his best friend from college, noticed this, too.

"My dad was my biggest hero and was really my best friend through high school. I remember seeing pain on Jonathan's face when I talked about my dad that way and there were times I would cut myself short from saying everything I wanted to say about my dad because he didn't have that relationship with his dad."

Jonathan said as an adult he reached out to his dad three different times, asking him for a closer relationship.

"The first time I was 18 yrs old and a freshman at Liberty. I wrote to him and voiced my concerns on paper about our relationship and told him I wanted us to be closer. And there was no response. The second time I was living in New York City going to cosmetology school and working as a sales clerk at Radio City Music Hall. I was bitter toward him for different events in my life. And I asked again for a close relationship, and still ... there was silence. And the third and final time was when I was a father, at 26 or 27 years old. It still ate at me, this divide between my father and me. I somehow got up the nerve to call him and tell him I wanted us to have a close relationship. He seemed to be in denial that there

*was anything wrong on his part. He told me that
I always get upset when I place high expectations
on things, and they didn't go the way I want them
to. And at the close of that conversation he said,
'You are grown now and have your own life and
I have mine.'*

"*Those words cut me to the core and that was
my last and final time to address this with him
again. At the moment I slammed shut forever my
heart with its hurts, unmet expectations and desire
to ever try again. The resentment I felt turned into
a deep seed of bitterness that I pushed way down
inside me. I laid it down and moved on with my
life and continued to be to my son the kind of dad
I wished my dad had been to me.*"

That bitterness and unforgiveness would be a hurdle to
Jonathan gaining victory over the Secret Place — and a hurdle
that would have to be overcome if God were going to use him
in a powerful testimony to His love and mercy.

But that hard spot in his heart did not soften before he
received the sobering news that he would be suffering a fatal
illness. He did not want to tell his parents he was HIV positive,
until a close friend of his encouraged him to. Oddly enough, the
opportunity came at a time when he was performing in a church
play and his parents had come to visit.

"*I didn't want to tell them. I didn't want to
feel my dad's judgment and I didn't want to see
my mother cry. I was performing in a passion play
at a local church. I was playing the part of Barab-*

bas. So I called my mom and dad and invited them for a visit to see this play. I told them over the phone that there was something I wanted to talk to them about when they were here. My mom kept saying, 'Talk about what?' I told her it was something that had to be said in person and I would talk to them when they got here.

"I don't think I have ever been more nervous in my life than when I sat down to tell my mom and dad. I was getting ready for another performance that evening, so that afternoon I asked my mom and dad to come sit at the round kitchen table, that I needed to talk to them. As they sat down, I excused myself quickly to the bathroom down the hallway. I shut the door and my nerves were shot. I started crying in the bathroom and quickly had to pull myself together.

"I came back to this round table. I was on one side, and across from me was my dad to my left and my mom beside him. I looked at them and said, 'Well, I don't know where to start.' I began to weep and couldn't gather my composure. My mother got up from the table and came around to me and hugged me and tried to comfort me. She began crying and that tore my heart. Finally I pulled myself together to speak. I told them that I had been infected with the HIV virus and that I was now HIV Positive.

"Up until this point there had never been one conversation about me being gay; it was never

spoken of. Through my tears, I could see my
mom's heart breaking for me. My dad was very
stoic and showed no outward emotion. He looked
at me and said, 'Well son, did you get this from a
man or a woman?' I looked down at the table and
said, 'I'd rather not say.' My dad quickly replied,
'Well son, you just gave me the answer.'

"As I had expected, I felt the very uncomfort-
able confrontation of my dad's judgment. He then
looked at me across the table; I lifted my swollen,
tear-stained eyes to his and he said, 'Sin bites,
doesn't it son.'

"All hell blew through me in that moment.
Satan had pulled up the years of deep-seeded
bitterness and unforgiveness I had buried and
flashed it right in front of my face. I got up from
the table and told my parents I had to head to the
church for the performance.

"Being an actor, I was able to get into my
character of Barabbas and put my own personal
character aside and made it through the performance. My parents left early the next morning and
I told them of my plans to hide this as long as I
could. I shared with them my fears of losing
everything I owned if anyone found out. We had
agreed not to even tell my siblings. I think for my
parents it was much easier to live in a state of
denial and not face what was really happening
with their son."

Jimmy and Rose remember that visit in 2000 well.

"I don't think he could have told us anything that would have been more heartbreaking than that," his mother said in 2009. "Knowing what he faced ... and of course at that time we had no idea anyway; this is our new knowledge of everything ... we had no idea that he was in that kind of lifestyle. It was very shocking."

"I was grieved that I could have a son that would go that direction after all the training he's had," his father added. "And I was angry about it — I wasn't angry at Jonny, but I was mad at the devil. ... Jonny was broken. We just encouraged him at that point, told him all the things I would tell anybody about how a person gets his life in order with the Lord: it's no major secret; it's just a matter of dealing with sin on a daily basis and staying in the Word and in prayer and in fellowship with other Christians — that's victory in any situation."

But Jonathan knew to deal with the sin he also had to deal with the lingering bitterness he had toward his father. "It wasn't until God shined His floodlight on my heart and revealed many years of bitterness and unforgiveness toward my dad, that I had real freedom; it all was linked to my heart," he said.

A few years later, Jonathan made one simple gesture that would make all the difference.

CHAPTER 5
Renovation

An artist when it comes to styling hair and making music come alive, it's no surprise that Jonathan likes his home to reflect his creative side.

When he bought a house of his own, he was always at work trying to decide how he could turn a boring living room into a personal movie theater, an old bathroom into a spa and a backyard into an outdoor paradise.

"Remodeling has always been a passion of mine," he said. "I've always been fascinated with taking something old and making it new, or taking something ordinary and making it extraordinary. ... Being in the hair business for the past 26 years, I am trained to look at a face and then visualize the finished product before ever executing the cut and color."

Linda Nell Cooper, a friend of his from college who has also directed him in many community theater productions over the years, said he has a creative eye.

"He's able to put things of color, shape and texture together and bring a beauty to something that everyone else thought was unnoticeable and dull."

When Jonathan bought a home in January 2000, he immediately started a renovation.

"My eyeballs were jumping around with all the endless possibilities. Even though I am not a carpenter, I would design the remodel plan and pay a skilled carpenter to do the work. This home project was endless. One thing led to the next thing. I worked tirelessly on this home. I completely gutted the kitchen and master bath, redesigned all the interior and exterior lighting in the house."

But while Jonathan was busy with renovation projects during the first five years in his new home, God was — at the same time — doing His own renovation on Jonathan. God had a plan, too, but He didn't hire out anyone to do the jobs; after all, He was the Master Carpenter, the Master Builder of Jonathan's life.

"It was during the five-year renovation I felt God drawing me back again. I would stand strong and ultimately fall back into the Secret Place. God was slowly revealing to me the sin of bitterness and unforgiveness toward my dad as I was trying and making major attempts to live right. At almost the same time as I completed the home renovation, God was putting His finishing touches on me."

***

As Jonathan proudly completed the home renovation five years later, he felt a tug at his heart to make a gesture toward his dad that he hadn't done in several years. It was a simple gesture, but it started the ball rolling.

"Every year when I would go to the store to pick out a Father's Day card, I would search and search for the right card, but I was flooded by these cards that had wonderful sentiments on them for your dad, and I didn't share any of those sentiments. I would usually leave the store in tears, again feeling the pain of a broken relationship with my dad.

"One night just before Father's Day, 2005, I was up late and was flipping the channels and came across the end of this movie where the movie soundtrack was playing as it was showing the credits. Music has always been such a powerful tool. Somehow, music is able to instantly open your heart. This incredible orchestration I was hearing just lifted my spirit to an incredible height; it was almost heavenly. Immediately I began to praise the Father in my heart, and that is when God used that moment to speak to me. Lovingly, the Holy Spirit spoke to my heart about the bitterness and unforgiveness toward my dad.

"I remember crying and just being honest with God. I said, 'Father, I know this thing with my dad is not good, I can't change it. I've tried; it's just not possible.' But God was not concerned

*with that relationship at the moment, but rather
He was convicting me of the status of my heart,
one filled with many, many years of unforgiveness
and resentment toward my dad.*

*"It seemed an impossible mountain to climb,
but with a pure heart I prayed, 'Father, I know
this is wrong and that I need to forgive ... I'm not
there yet, but will you please take the desire I have
to forgive and somehow grow it.' I went to sleep
that night and slept like a baby.*

*"Father's Day was still approaching and still I
was resolved not to send a card that year. I just
thought, 'Why bother?' A few nights later, I had
a dream, one of those dreams that is crystal clear
in every detail — the kind of dream that stays with
you for days. In my dream I was at a wake for a
deceased relative — my dad. All of my family was
there and seated and no one had the strength to
start the line to view the body. Everyone was
crying and sobbing. I was upset that my dad was
gone, but I didn't feel the level of the connection to
him that my family did, so I thought, well, I will
start the line. I was certainly sad that in the dream
my dad was gone, but I knew I could start the line
for my family. As I stood up and was walking
toward the casket, there was a closed door to my
right. I looked and saw my dad in his spirit body
come through the door. No one else in my dream
was aware of this except for me. I looked and my
dad looked young and full of life. He appeared the*

age he was when I was a little boy. As if in a movie, the scene began to zoom in slowly on his eyes. It was amazing. My dad's eyes sparkled with life, but more than that, I could see for the first time the incredible love he had for me. I woke up from this dream with tears in my eyes. I was smiling and just soaking in this dream. How awesome this was, that I felt and saw in my dad's eyes his love for me, his son. As I became more awake, I realized how wonderful this all was, but snapping back to reality I thought, 'It was only a dream.'

"But it was way more than that. God was using all this to soften my heart. He was at work honoring my request to take my desire to forgive and make it grow. Not only did I send a Father's Day card that year, I handmade a special card. I dug through old pictures and found a shot of my dad holding me in his arms when I was a baby. I scanned it and made my dad a card and sent it to him. And I didn't stop there. I love pictures and like to scan them and put in different frames around my home, but nowhere in my house did I display a picture of my dad and I together. For the first time, I scanned this picture and proudly displayed it on my mantle.

"A couple of weeks later, I received a phone call from my mom asking me if I was going to be home, and that they were thinking about coming up to visit me and my son. There was not a word spoken about the card. When they came, we went out to eat one night. My dad and my son went to park the car and my mom and I went in to get a table. It didn't even cross my mind this time to pick where I would sit. See, in the past whenever we would go out to eat, I always made sure I was not sitting directly across from my dad. I would sit to the side of him or at the end of the table. It just felt too confrontational for me to be directly in front of him. But this time, because we were seated at different times, my mom and I were on one side and my son and dad were across from us. And I was directly in front of my dad's face.

"This time together was very, very different to me. My dad and I who in the past rarely communicated all of the sudden were having wonderful conversation. I was telling him stories and making him laugh. Wow, this was incredible. Then something even more incredible happened. While I was in the middle of a sentence talking, it was as if for a few seconds God supernaturally lowered the veil. This time, not in a dream but physically, I saw in my dad's eyes this amazing love for me. It was as if in those few seconds time stood still. My dad was less than two feet in front of me and I saw this sparkle of love in his eyes for me. And it took my breath, I could hardly speak and finish my sentence.

"In that instant, God answered my prayer. He had taken my desire to forgive and made it grow. When I saw this love in my dad's eyes, with God's help, He instantly removed a lifetime of bitterness, resentment, and unforgiveness in my heart towards my dad. God was placing in my heart an agape love for my dad. I know now my dad has always loved me, but I believe early on Satan somehow blocked me from seeing this love.

"We finished eating dinner that night and then I treated them to ice cream. It was just so unlike any other visit, my dad and I were actually talking to one another and enjoying each other's company. After they left and drove back to Memphis, the events of this day were etched in my mind and heart. My dad has always been sort of a skeptic of experiences with dreams so I thought I'd sit on this a while and see if it was real. After all, it was my dad who was famous for saying, 'Time will tell.'

"I waited two or three months, then I finally decided to e-mail my dad and share with him these amazing events that had taken place. God had most definitely taken my desire to forgive and grew it until I could completely let it go. The first thing I noticed was that when I would look at a picture of my dad after that, there were no longer bad feelings or sadness at not being close. There was a genuine love free of bitterness and unforgiveness. I no longer felt the need to bring up hurts from the past; it was over, gone, washed away."

Up until the forgiveness, Jonathan was hiding in the Secret Place. But when the forgiveness happened in his heart, he desired to leave it behind — permanently. "It was at that time I felt the Holy Spirit really take over and for the first time I was 'completely His,'" he said.

This change in Jonathan's heart was not something he could hide. It was apparent to family, friends and even his customers at the salon.

Gale Purvis, a fairly new customer at the time, said she sensed a "heaviness" about him a couple years before. She couldn't put her finger on it, but she decided to pray for him. Then, a year later, she saw his countenance change — he was no longer "downcast," she said. "I told him, 'Something good is going on in your life.' He laughed and said, 'Yes there was, that he had fallen away from the Lord but now he was back.'" He didn't tell her then, but invited her to Thomas Road Baptist Church to hear his testimony a couple months later. "That was the neatest, most wonderful testimony ... I say to him now that he seems so free; he's at a peace where a lot of people want to be."

Carolyn Fitzgerald, a customer for more than more than 20 years, could tell the difference, too. She said his story of forgiveness can be a lesson for all.

"He has demonstrated to me by example that he can forgive people; he can love people and truly forgive them — not the kind you do with lip service, but the kind where you really do forgive — and that is one of the hardest things you'll ever do."

Longtime friend Marie Achilles can attest to Jonathan's renovation. She first met Jonathan when he went on a short-term mission trip to Europe that her husband Doug conducted through Liberty Baptist College. She saw Jonathan's caring heart even then, as he sang and served in that ministry as a college student. And she saw that caring heart years later when Doug fell ill to cancer and was bedridden for 15 months. Jonathan would come cut Doug's hair then sit by his bedside, tell stories and sing to him. Marie and Doug were two of the very few people who knew of Jonathan's call to go public. Doug died before he could see the impact of that night, but Marie, who was out of town at the time, heard the service on the radio.

"I do believe when he sang at that church that night, that was the strongest I've heard him sing. This time it was powerful ... it was a ministry that night that I had never heard Jonathan do."

Marie said after Jonathan learned he had AIDS, he embraced the life God had given him and she was proud to see him begin ministering to others in an even bigger way.

"He's always been Jonny ... he's just a better version of Jonny now."

Many people who knew Jonathan as a child had the chance to see this "better version" when he was asked to give his testimony at his hometown church near Memphis, Tenn., on Aug. 24, 2008, a whole nine months after he had gone public with his news at Thomas Road Baptist Church.

In an ironic twist to his life story, he would be giving his testimony from behind the same pulpit where his father had preached many years ago.

As he stood at that pulpit — with his father sitting in a pew — it was a reversal of roles that neither of them could have ever imagined. But there he was, speaking in front of his family and many of the same people who had watched him grow up at Broadway Baptist Church.

No, it wasn't anything like the other Broadway he had imagined would make him a star years ago, but it *was* a chance for him to shine — not his own light, but the light of the Heavenly Father, the One who had reached down to pull him out of a world of darkness.

Jonathan began by welcoming everyone there, saying what a privilege it was to have been invited back to the church that holds so many wonderful memories for him. But then the real renovation of his heart showed when he started his talk by welcoming two special guests.

> *"This morning I wanted to honor two very special people in my life. They are responsible for two things: number one, they are responsible for my physical being because they gave me life. These two people that I want you to help me honor and thank today are responsible for me being here sharing this story of God's redemption with you. You see, they believed a promise in Proverbs: God said if you would raise your children in the way they should go, when they're older they won't depart from it. Ladies and gentlemen, please help me welcome and publicly honor my parents, Rose and Jimmy Ervin."*

When the applause died down, he continued to talk about his Christian home and biblical upbringing; he wanted people to know where he had come from, that he was someone just like them sitting in those pews many years earlier, but he was also "a sinner saved by grace."

"It was an emotional time for the whole family," his mother recalls. "This is the first time for us to sit there and listen to his story, with our friends all around us, so it was an emotional thing."

It was especially emotional for Jonathan. At one point he had to take a deep breath and hold back the tears. That's when he was talking about his father and how he would encourage his children to memorize Scripture as a way to earn money.

"That was very smart because what he was doing was hiding the word of God — that promises not to return void — in the hearts of his children, and," as Jonathan said, getting choked up and fighting back the tears, " ... thank you for that, Dad."

It touched Jimmy Ervin's heart to hear his son say those words and to see him testify to God's work in his life.

As it turns out, the Ervins had tickets to a ballgame out of town that day, but when they found out that was when Jonathan was speaking, they made the trip to see him instead.

"We wanted to support Jonny there and a lot of the people who knew Jonny from a little boy and love Jonny and still do were there," he said.

That included Bobby Moore, the church's former pastor when the Ervin family was there many years ago. He remembers those years well.

"The whole family was involved in the ministry with their dad. They were dearly loved in our church. Our church had some of its greatest days when they were there," he said.

And he remembers a young, outgoing and friendly Jonny, but knew there were problems even then.

"As I observed Jonny he always felt a sense of insecurity ... I don't think he ever had a recognition of value in life because he didn't know who he was in Christ," Moore said. And with Jonny's father, "things were black and white," he said, which didn't bother Moore, but he could tell Jonny rebelled against that.

But when he reunited with the Ervins that day in 2008, it was all a different story. And Jonny was much different, too. Moore said Jonny's testimony was powerful.

"I felt like he took responsibility for his life; he didn't blame other people; he demonstrated some genuine brokenness and repentance over his lifestyle," he said. "I felt like there was a deep humility when he shared it; it wasn't bragging ... he was very straightforward."

It caused Moore and many others to shower him with an unconditional love that day. "I certainly didn't think any less of him," his former pastor said. "He was just like scads of people I've dealt with (with other addictions) and I knew his need wasn't too big for the Lord — and He sure proved that."

Jimmy Ervin said he has never felt embarrassment for his son's story — only praise for a God who was bringing glory to Himself through Jonathan's changed life.

"We would not be embarrassed for any person to talk about victory they have in Christ," he said. "That's what it's about; it's about a person getting victory and there's nothing too hard for God to do; nothing is impossible for God."

That's why it was possible for Jonathan to stand in that same spot his father had many years ago and speak about a lifestyle no one would have ever thought the "preacher's kid" would have

fallen into. But he did. And by the Master Renovator's hand —
and the prayers of his faithful parents — he was redeemed.

"I believe whatsoever God does, He does forever," said his
father Jimmy Ervin. "God answered our prayers ... because Jonny
has come full circle; he's not come back without scars, but he's
come back ... and the scars will always be there and those are
God's reminders."

Jonny &
Dad
1962

Jonny,
3 years old

Pam, Mike, Jonny
& Penny

1st Place Talent Show Winner,
12th Grade, 1980

Jonny
Senior Portrait

Hair Cut Sign-up Sheet
in Liberty University Dorm

72

College Best Friends
Curt Motsinger & David Barstead

JONNY ERVIN
Memphis, Tennessee

smite
STUDENT MISSIONARY INTERN TRAINING for EVANGELISM

Ministry of Thomas Road Baptist Church
Lynchburg, VA 24514

Prayer Card for smite
European Team

Children of Greece
Mission Trip

JOHNNY ERVIN
STUDENT NAME

6-82-123 BH
IDENTIFICATION #

9/83
EXPIRATION DATE

STUDENT'S SIGNATURE

NOT VALID FOR
CASHING CHECK

Robert Fiance School of Hair Design,
NYC 1982

*Wedding of
Jonny &
Ellen*
1986

*First Embrace
of Son Shaun
Ervin, 1987*

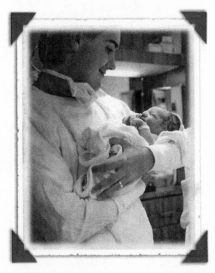

Birthday for Shaun

Family Vacation

Father/Son Trip Out West

Sibling

Reunion

2000

Before the Home Makeover
414 Lake Vista Drive

After the Home Makeover

Production of CATS
E.C. Glass High School, 2006

Filmed
Testimony
with Charles
Billingsley

Going Public
Thomas Road Baptist Church, 2007

Prayer of Dedication
by Daniel Henderson

Dad, Jonny & Mom
Parents' 50th Wedding Anniversary

"Adopted Lynchburg Mom"
Sandy Bradshaw

81

*Father &
Son*
2008

College Friend Linda Randle
at the Gaither Concert, 2009

CHAPTER 6
The Finish Line

Jonathan admits he has never been athletic. And winning a race was certainly not something he would ever achieve in life. But once God's renovation of his heart took place, Jonathan was able to get on the mark for the race of his life — one where he would never allow defeat ever again.

***

A couple of years before Jonathan found out he was HIV positive, he remembers one of the times he cried out to God to take away the same-sex attraction.

"I remember having a contrite heart and lifting a very sobering prayer to God: 'Father, whatever it takes for me not to miss Heaven, I am willing.' Little did I know the power of that prayer.

Did God strike me with AIDS? Of course not. But has He used this in my life to bring me to a place of true repentance, turning away from a life that doesn't please him? Absolutely."

When Jonathan attended Liberty Baptist College, he became close friends with the dean of men, Dane Emerick, who now serves in the University's Student Care office and counsels students who struggle with sexual identity. Emerick said people must realize, "God does not create bad things, but bad things happen," and that "God is a good thing in life when bad things happen."

"I look at this and I realize that God is a good thing in Jonny's life even through this bad that's going on (AIDS)," he said. "Obviously God has used it as a messenger in his life to bring him back to a right relationship with Himself and I believe Jonny's having that intimate relationship with the Lord."

Jonathan says he's always had a heart for God, but never had the "sticking power" to not return to the Secret Place. It was only after God completed the renovation of his heart, once filled with bitterness toward his dad, that he felt the Holy Spirit take over.

"As I was learning to surrender areas of my life to Him, I witnessed a real thing," he said. "The Holy Spirit was giving me the power to live a life that would honor Him, a power over my desires of the flesh."

But for Jonathan, that didn't mean he had won the race — he still had many laps to go and many hurdles along the way, but he was gaining ground each time he resisted temptation.

"Do I still have same-sex attraction? Of course I do. Am I still tempted to go back to my homosexual lifestyle? Sometimes.

But my strength has come totally from God. God loves me as I am, flaws and all, but here's the difference: it has only been through the power of the Holy Spirit that He has totally empowered me to live a pure life that honors the Father.

"I used to cry endless tears begging God to take away my same-sex attraction, because if He would do this for me, then I could live a pure life. That prayer and focus are no longer a part of my prayers. I have learned to trust completely what God has done in my heart. Yes all the temptations and desires are still there, but the strength not to act upon them comes from above ... from a personal relationship with Christ.

"The Bible says if you will resist temptation, God is faithful to make a way of escape for you. God has taught me He is for our success: 'He is too wise to ever make a mistake, and too kind to ever hurt you.' God showed me His amazing love for me right where I was at — a backslidden sinner. He loved me and accepted me as I was."

But God never promises a life without temptation, Emerick said, quoting 2 Corinthians 5:17: "Therefore if any man is in Christ, he is a new creature; the old things are passed away; behold, new things have come."

"If you read that verse and follow through on it, you discover what that verse is saying," he said, "that I'm a new creature, this is not a part of my nature, but yet the old things I am passing by and they're still calling me and I have to keep walking, with tunnel vision, and fixing my eyes on Jesus Christ."

When runners are circling a track, doing the number of laps required for a race, they pass by the same sights off the track over and over again. If a runner was to take his eyes off the track before him and focus instead on something off to the side — still running — their head would eventually turn, then their shoulders, then their torso and then the rest of their body, until they were running backward, further and further from the finish line.

That's not what Jonathan wanted to do, so he took his eyes off those sights — in some cases, literally.

> *"Before and during the renovation process of my own soul, if I would fall into temptation I would feel so beat up, defeated, shamed and great conviction. God showed me that I had to seek Him first in everything I did. For example, hiding in the Secret Place for many secret gay people is the Internet. It's private, no one sees you, and yet you are feeding this part of temptation with sin. As my relationship with God got stronger, I quit looking at Internet porn, I quit going to places out of town where I knew I could find male companionship, I quit visiting gay chat rooms.*
>
> *"I began listening to the Bible on my iPod, just to hear God's word speaking to my heart and I found great strength in that. I also listen to Christian music while I exercise. There is a song that has become my anthem as I look toward Heaven and run this race to the finish line. On Charles Billingsley's album, 'Mark of a Mission,' he recorded a song called 'Finish Strong.' These lyrics have inspired me:*
>
> *'It's not about how fast I run/It's not about how far I've come/It's all about the moment when*

I hear, "My child, well done"/I wanna finish strong, though the road is long/Crossing that line and still pressin on/ I want to finish strong, faithful to the Father/ .... Oh I want to finish strong.'

"Praise and worship has become a big part of my daily life, whether in the car or on the treadmill or walking around the lake near my house. Good, uplifting music puts my thoughts on God and Heaven. As I look up to the sky toward Heaven, I say out loud, 'Your cross before me, the world behind me, still I will follow, no turning back, no turning back.'"

Jonathan says turning back, after he's experienced the incredible work of God in his life, would be the most foolish thing he could do. "Nothing of that lifestyle compares," he told host Terry Meeuwsen on the "Living the Life" TV talk show on CBN in November 2008. He called it "a counterfeit of love."

"Make no mistake there is a great allure and attraction to the gay lifestyle. God even says in the Bible that sin is fun ... for a season. But it is God's law that we will reap what we have sewn.

"It (the temptation) is not so much on my mind now as before because I have filled my mind, my sight, and my hearing with things that honor God. My focus is totally on Heaven and spending eternity with the one who has redeemed my soul at Calvary. I'm so thankful God made a provision for all mankind to have eternal life through Jesus Christ."

Heaven ... eternity ... the finish line.

Anyone who had the chance to spend any time with Jonathan after his diagnosis knows that eternity was more real to him than it was to most people. But it wasn't just because his doctor told him he had six to 12 months to live, but because he had a longing to see this "perfect place" he had heard so much about.

> "When I was a small child, my dad would sit me at the kitchen table and would share with me wonderful stories about heaven and how the Bible describes this place, a place God is preparing for us who believe in His son Jesus Christ. And I'm reminded how the Bible teaches: blessed are those who have never seen and yet believe. (John 20:29)

> "I've always been completely captured by stories of near-death experiences and the stories told about these encounters. I've never seen an angel, or heard God's audible voice. It's always been my prayer that I will have an incredible story to share with those present when I'm on my death bed. A story like that takes flight and is told over and over. Those stories have always somehow increased my faith."

Jonathan often talks about heaven in casual conversation. He talks about living with God for eternity, with no pain or suffering or inner struggles, and about seeing people he knows who have gone on before him.

"I think I have such a understanding of the soul and the spirit and that it lives on beyond this physical body, forever," he said.

Jonathan shared his testimony one day with a woman whose premature twin baby girls died at birth. When she shared her own story with him, he immediately asked her, "What's their names? You know I'll be seeing them before you will. I can't wait to meet them. It's wonderful there, you know."

Jonathan was so sure of this wonderful place called heaven that after he found out he had AIDS, he purchased a burial plot, ordered his own gravestone and had it installed there. He has even taken family members and close friends by to see it and has taken pictures of them there, beside the spot where his earthly body will lie someday. Some people may think it odd that he has such peace at what should be such a tumultuous time.

> *"The question I get from most people is, 'Are you afraid?' Yes, I'm afraid of suffering because I don't like pain. But I'm not afraid of being at the end of my life. It's weird — when you are at the end of your life, you almost know. It's not like I feel like I've been cheated out of years, there's just a peace — a peace you cannot explain — and there is excitement in me that I cannot wait to get there.*
>
> *"Having such a perspective on life, our spirit and soul within us, and eternity ... it has given me peace to know I am following God's way to live. God's plan for how we are to live is not designed for us not to have fun, but in return He truly gives a peace and a joy — deep in your soul — that only*

comes from above. I know this to be true, I have found the secret to life: following Christ 100 percent … all the way to the finish line."

CHAPTER 7
Season Of Opportunity

Jonathan Ervin had a love for the stage since childhood. His potential was seen early on when he won a school talent show — year after year. In college, he sang for ministry teams and even took his talented voice through Europe.

Jonathan also learned to play the piano — by ear. Everything about music just came naturally to him. But hitting the notes with his voice is what he loved most.

Being third in the birth order in his home, a young Jonathan longed for something that could really take him places. His sisters and brother had their own activities they excelled in and he wanted to find his niche, too.

"My sister Pam, the oldest, was the golden child who was perfect in every way to me; she played the piano. Mike, my older brother, played sports, and Penny, the youngest, was an amazing basketball player. And then there was Jonny, who was awkward, bony-skinny, and did not really have any accomplishments."

That was, until he learned he could sing.

***

Jonathan's oldest sister Pam remembers the very day he discovered his gift.

"My dad was preaching in a small country church. They had dinner on the grounds all afternoon. They had to use a sound system and when Jonny heard his voice on the microphone he was just amazed; he'd never heard his voice amplified before."

Then there was the time his parents heard him — in the back seat of their station wagon.

"I remember one time riding in the station wagon with all four of us kids in the back and we were all singing," he said. "There was a lady in our church who had an amazing voice and I started imitating the way she sang. I will never forget my dad saying, 'Jonny, I believe the Lord may be giving you a singing talent.' Little did he know the power of those words to me."

Jonathan even struck a chord with that outdoorsy, athletic brother of his.

"I will cry like a baby hearing him sing a song — I don't care what it is — it can be 'Jesus Loves Me,' but his emotion and tone he puts into that just touches me," Mike Ervin said.

Jonathan also remembers the day someone outside of his family noticed his talent.

"One day after school I was in the chorus room, playing the piano and singing my heart

out, like you do in the shower when you know
no one else is listening. And another student
walked in and I quickly stopped. He said, 'Was
that you singing in here?' I was embarrassed and
reluctantly said 'Yes.' This student got so excited
and couldn't believe that came out of me. He told
me I needed to audition for the school talent
show. I thought there was no way I could stand
in front of 1,000 people and sing. But with that
student's encouragement I auditioned. That big
night came, the gym was packed, bleachers and
the floor. I grabbed the mic and the spotlights
were on me. No one knew I could sing and
couldn't believe the voice came out of me. That
night I won first place.

"Finally, all of the sudden, everyone in the
school knew who Jonny Ervin was. The jocks who
were brutally cruel to me all of the sudden noticed
that the cheerleaders and all the popular kids were
saying my name. And now the jocks were allowing me into their circle because all the girls were
wanting to be around me and were huge fans. I
went on to win first place in the talent show every
year until I graduated."

It did huge things for his self-esteem. He soon learned to
love the stage. Being out in front wasn't so scary anymore. His
passion to be heard by an audience grew stronger every day.
When he ventured to New York City during his college years,
it grew even stronger.

"In 1982 when I was living in NYC and working at Radio City Music Hall, the excitement was intense being around professionals in show business. This was my dream to make it in music. I remember one night after selling bar tickets for a concert, it was after midnight, the music hall was closed and all the lights were out inside the theater except one light beaming down on the lonely, empty center stage.

"I remember as I was going to change back into my street clothes from my work uniform, I walked out onto the center stage. No one was in the music hall except for a few mice and probably roaches scavenging around for a piece of popcorn or candy on the floor of the auditorium. I remember singing the song "Memory" from the Broadway musical "CATS" that was playing in NYC while I was living there. I belted the song out with all my heart. I remember looking up into heaven and praying, 'Father, please let me perform one day on this stage before I die'."

But that would never happen. After returning to Lynchburg, Va., he became content doing some music ministry and community theater. He played many different roles, from Old Deuteronomy in "CATS," to musicals where he was the youthful cad, the flirt, or the wholesome boy next door. His friend Linda Nell Cooper, from his college days, was still in Lynchburg and ended up directing him in several productions. She said his gift was always obvious.

"His gift is a passion for music and his ability to communicate that passion when he sings. It's a love for the lyrics, how he communicates them, how it comes across to the audience — you get caught up in that love as well," she said.

Standing on a stage seemed to be what Jonathan Ervin was meant for, or at least he thought so, until many years later when it was time for him to answer God's call to go public with the secret lifestyle he had been leading most of his adult life. Suddenly he did not care to be in front of everyone. The embarrassment and shame would far outweigh the attention he could receive by doing this, he said. At first, he wanted to stay far away from the idea. But when the call on his life grew stronger, he knew what he had to do. But telling the people who had known him all his life what he was about to do would be a big hurdle, especially since they had known him all his life as someone who had wanted to be in the spotlight.

"When Jonny realized he had talent and could sing, the attention he got from that was big — (he thought) Barry Manilow was nothing next to him. He appeared selfish to most people ... Jonny was about Jonny," his brother Mike recalls.

But this time would be different, for sure, and he would have to learn to step out of the spotlight so God could get all the glory.

Even some close friends and family admit they weren't sure his calling was "real" at first, knowing how Jonathan always loved an audience. But as he let the doors swing wide open by themselves, allowing him to share his testimony and sing, people began to see that Jonathan was not after any applause this time around.

Bobby Moore, Jonathan's pastor growing up, was there when Jonathan returned to his home church to testify to God's goodness in his life.

"I felt like he took responsibility for his life; he didn't blame other people. He demonstrated some genuine brokenness and repentance over his lifestyle," Moore said. "I felt like there was a deep humility when he shared it; it wasn't bragging."

It seemed he was heeding his big brother's advice:

"(I told him) stand down, let Christ be at the center of everything you say — anything you say, anything you do, what you sing —make sure it brings glory to Him, not you," Mike Ervin said. "You can stand up and talk about your darkness, but everything needs to bring light to His glory. From this point on in your life, or however long it goes, it's going to be because God's going to get glory or it's going to reach other people through your testimony."

The doors that opened for Jonathan were huge. After a magazine article ran in the "Liberty Journal," with 300,000 copies distributed across the country to alumni, pastors and anyone connected with Liberty University, Jonathan began receiving requests for interviews. Still, he had to keep perspective.

Curt Motsinger, his best friend from college, was one of the first people Jonathan told about his desire to share his testimony publicly. Knowing Jonathan well, but also being in the ministry himself, he wanted to keep his friend's motives in check.

"I wanted to make sure that it wasn't just a limelight kind of thing, that he really wanted to serve. I wanted to make sure that he really was wanting to do whatever God was leading him to do," Motsinger said. "I basically told him, 'You need to do whatever they want you to do, maybe be willing to help counsel, rather than being up front or that sort of thing.' He seemed to be willing to do whatever. I really was pleasantly impressed that he was heading in the right direction with that."

Jonathan's old youth pastor even chimed in, urging him to be careful how he handled the media attention and warning him to not get tossed around in all the differing views.

"I warned him about being taken advantage of ... about being the 'media puppet for the moment' ... the 'Christian puppet for the moment' and to protect himself from that," said Mark Gold, who is now a missions pastor in Minnesota, in a twin cities suburb. "But he's definitely carrying an important message to an important group of people who need to know they're loved and cared about."

Gold, who describes his own church as a "hospital" of sorts for broken souls, says he was not surprised by Jonny's admission, even after knowing him as a "pastor pleaser" so many years ago. Gold said he has met and counseled many Christians who have a past like Jonathan's and in hearing and reading about Jonathan's story, he can tell there's been a change for the better.

"Everybody I know that's had a genuine touch from God is honest about their sin past," he said. "Ex-adulterers, ex-pornographers, ex-gamblers ... they're all being real honest about their ugly past because it's all been forgiven. Jonathan's admission is not any different to me than a gal who's been in the occult or a guy who's committed adultery or drug used. I just rejoiced with Jonny that he could go public with that. I'm excited about what Jonny's doing, and I hope he can build a bridge to a community that doesn't think Christians care about them."

Even though Jonathan had a desire to share his life struggles "to help others who are hiding in the Secret Place," he still
decided he would sit back and allow God to open the doors for
him. That's why when Julie Jenney, managing producer of
"Living the Life" — a talk show on Pat Robertson's Christian
Broadcasting Network — called to invite him to Virginia Beach
to be on the show, he quickly accepted. Jenney heard of
Jonathan through the magazine article and thought he would
make a wonderful, inspiring testimony for the show.

Jenney was in the control room the day Jonathan was being
interviewed by Terry Meeuwsen, co-host of the "700 Club." She
said the staff sees powerful testimonies every day, but they were
especially inspired by Jonathan's segment.

"It was interesting because I got immediate feedback from
people on the set and on the control room," Jenney said. "This
was a group of people who see a lot of stuff and see a lot of
stories. It's pretty mind-blowing when Jonathan talks about how
he should be sick; everyone was blown away with that. I would
say it's pretty miraculous, I think God is just using him."

To hear the story of a man with AIDS who is a "walking
miracle" is touching enough — but to hear that he is a Christian who once lived a homosexual lifestyle (and secret at that)
is another dimension of the story.

Santosh Y. Aghamkar, production manager of WLXI, a sister
station for TCT (Total Christian Television) out of Greensboro,
N.C., had received the "Liberty Journal" article as well and
knew immediately that he had to have Jonathan on "TCT
Alive," a talk show that airs by satellite in 180 countries.

"What I liked about him is ... being in that [gay] lifestyle he realized what was happening to him and how wrong it was and he had accepted Christ and he wanted to help others who are going through this struggle," Aghamkar said. "This kind of thing [homosexuality] is happening all over the world but people are shunned because of what they are going through instead of given care and love — and that's the message of Christ."

Like Jenney, he too said he gets lots of calls to interview different guests and hears lots of testimonies, "but Jonathan's story was unique because he had gone through all these things, and he had accepted Christ, and openly he's saying that was wrong what I did — and he's not only saying it is wrong but there is solution to it ... and he's leading them to that ... the answer they are looking for."

But Christians in the media announcing a secret gay lifestyle is nothing new to modern society. Newsrooms were buzzing all over the country when, in November 2006, Ted Haggard, the former leader of the National Association of Evangelicals and former pastor of the Colorado megachurch he founded confessed to sexual immorality. But Jonathan says Haggard's story "is about scandal and my story is about redemption. I think it is what God wants to be told to many who struggle with this."

Jonathan knew he was going against the flow in the secular world when he talked about his homosexual lifestyle as a sin. He knows there are people claiming to be Christians who are still living that lifestyle. How do they do it? "I don't know," Jonathan said. "I felt such strong conviction that it was wrong, so I really don't know what to think about that."

He does, however, know what ground he's standing on.

> "It's a time where society and the whole world is crying out to accept this as a normal lifestyle. Many gay activists would say I am denying myself and how I was created by God, that I was born this way and I have no choice in it. Again, my answer to that is we are all born into a sin nature. But it doesn't negate God's stand against sin, and He himself said homosexuality was an abomination against Him (Leviticus 18:22) and even went further to say homosexuals would not inherit God's kingdom. (1 Corinthians 6:9-10)
>
> "It's amazing how many good people will quickly adopt the world's view, but I think they forget God's word said: the road to Heaven is very narrow and few travel it, but that the road to hell is broad and there are many on it."

Since his first public testimony, Jonathan has never stopped short of saying he has same-sex attraction — he notices those tendencies full well. But, as he explained to a reporter off-air, after being interviewed for a segment on "The Controversial Ex-Gay Movement" on a Lynchburg TV station, "I could put all of my eggs in one of two baskets here. One, I could say, OK I'm going to stand before my creator — and I'm at the end of my life — and I can either embrace what the world says about it OR I said choose to put my eggs in this basket: believe God's word is true. So I've come to Him for forgiveness for this sin and I'm going to put all my eggs in that basket and that's my choice. If I'm making a mistake, I'm gonna make a mistake on believing God's word is true."

His strong convictions are what attracted independent film producer Kent Williamson, who wanted to include Jonathan in his film, "Stained Glass Rainbows," an exploration of the issues surrounding homosexuality and faith.

The film's lineup includes a wide variety of viewpoints, from a lesbian minister and members of the God Hates Fags movement, to theologians, people who lead ministries geared toward the homosexual population and "people like Jonathan who are just living their lives, but there's a wrestling match going on deep within their soul on how to live their faith," Williamson said.

Jonathan's story was remarkable and a must-have for the film, he said.

"Here we have someone who's been involved in the homosexual lifestyle for a long time, and yet his faith to him is more important than some identity he would even give himself, it's more important than a label that society might want to put on him. So when I see someone taking their faith that seriously, it's like 'Wow—this is an interesting story that needs to be told.'"

Williamson, who runs Paladin Pictures out of Charlottesville, Va., hopes Jonathan's redemption story will help spur conversation among Christians, and the conservative church in particular.

"I think this is a critical discussion and dialogue that needs to be taking place within the faith community because it is one that is extremely important," he said. "This issue, not only is it tearing denominations apart, it's tearing individual churches apart and it's tearing families apart. So I think it's very important conversation for the church to be engaged in."

If this is true, then Jonathan's testimonies at churches from Ohio to Alabama to Virginia are a step in the right direction.

Steve Bell first met Jonathan when he was a youth intern at Jonathan's home church near Memphis, Tenn. When he, too, had read the magazine article and recognized Jonathan as being that teenage boy he remembered, he got back in touch with him and invited him to speak at Flint River Baptist Church near Huntsville, Ala., where he is the pastor.

Not unlike many of the pastors and even TV producers who had sought out Jonathan for his testimony, Bell said he was nervous.

"I didn't know how the people would receive him — this is the deep south. A lot of times I think believers can very easily not only hate the sin but hate the sinner as well," Bell said. "But he came and did an awesome job — we had so many different responses from different people over the next days and weeks."

Those responses, Bell said, "included a lady who commented how much God had spoken to her heart because one of her daughters was a homosexual and that just gave her a whole new light of understanding. There was another lady, a senior citizen, who commented how God had changed her whole outlook and that she was going to be a lot more compassion-focused and no longer look at homosexuals as just a group of people, but as individuals who had needs — that was huge for her.

"A young married man made the comment that he thought it was one of the greatest services we ever had there in the church and a couple of college kids, it encouraged them to reach out to a transsexual at their college who was planning to have gender surgery. Through talking and reaching out to him, he eventually agreed to come to church with them and he prayed to receive Christ. It was really good to see Jonathan's story had an impact on all the different age groups."

Dale Seley, pastor of Downtown Baptist Church in Alexandria, Va., said Jonathan is on his church's weekly prayer list.

"We pray for him regularly that God will sustain his health and in doing so, this is creating a bond between our church family and Jonathan."

Jonathan has received cards and e-mails from church members and from many other people who have heard his testimony, some from people who have not dealt with HIV or homosexuality, but have been impacted by his story nonetheless.

A woman in her 20s visited Ervin near Christmastime at the salon where he worked. It had been about a month after he had first gone public with his testimony. The woman was a former client of Jonathan's. She immediately hugged him, gave him a card and left. He read it later; it said that someone had e-mailed her his testimony and it touched her.

"She said, 'I was ready to tell my husband I didn't love him anymore, ready to end my marriage.' She said, 'Here I was ready to toss all this away,'" Jonathan recalls. After seeing his testimony, the woman wrote she had realized life "is really about your family and your relationship with God" and she changed her mind.

Students at Liberty University have approached Jonathan and told him that his testimony was their testimony. After the convocation where he sang and shared with the college's entire student body, a female student told him about a friend struggling with homosexuality and wanted to know if he could help.

His son Shaun, a Liberty University student at the time, even tells of a fellow student who wanted to meet him after she read the magazine article about his dad and learned there was someone else like herself at Liberty — her dad had been involved in a homosexual lifestyle as well.

Jonathan said he has made friends since his first testimony and his old friendships are even stronger. That includes the ties with his family.

His brother Mike said Jonathan's life has had a major impact on his own walk with Christ.

"While it is apparent Jonny's life may have been diagnosed with a certain conclusion, what excuse am I giving to not take my stance for Christ? Jonny's reality has only inspired me to no longer take for granted my life, but to be more determined to bear my cross."

Mike shares a special memory from their childhood.

> "When we were young kids, we were at our aunt's home for a visit and were in the backyard; we decided to climb a tree. I went first and Jonny followed. He was hesitant, but determined to keep up. Twelve feet up into the tree Jonny got caught between branches. ... He shouted out, 'I can't do it.' I scurried back down some to help him. I said, 'Come on, give me your hand.' Reluctantly, he reached out. I could see his fright — he missed my grip. I watched him fall, hitting one branch on his way down, landing hard on a dog house below and rolling to the ground. I felt so helpless and to this day still remember the fear that consumed me. I

could do nothing but hurry to the ground, praying
to God: "Please, LORD!" I practically jumped
out of the tree wanting so desperately to be able to
reverse the moment that just took my breath away.

"Getting to the ground and begging Jonny to
speak, then recognizing his breath was knocked out
of him, he gasped for air. He laid there quietly for
a minute, sat up and said, 'I'm OK.' The relief
we both felt, no doubt looking back, was just one
more sure experience of angels watching over us.
As if one caught him and carefully protected his
fall and impact to the ground."

This memory, Mike said, best describes his feelings about his brother today, while he is dying of AIDS. "I want to help and protect my brother, but I am left to be totally dependant on God and His angels to protect Jonny while I watch and pray, 'Lord please!' You must believe me when I say again I see angels around him."

Jonathan was under God's protection, for sure, and knowing this he has grabbed hold of his season of opportunity — and hasn't let up.

His father says it is obvious from the many mail and e-mail responses Jonathan has received, that God is using his son in many lives. And, he adds, "we probably will not know everyone he's blessed or helped ... the people that don't respond."

His mother says she believes her son is reaching people now that others, even seasoned pastors, couldn't reach. His dad agrees.

"As the saying goes, you don't know how an Indian feels until you've walked in his moccasins before," Jimmy Ervin said.

And as far as Jonathan's ministry is concerned, his father, a seasoned pastor himself, said, "He's getting more ministry done now than he ever has in his whole life. He's a minister of the Gospel and God's using it."

CHAPTER 8
Power Of A Father's Love

When Jonathan was able to gain victory over his secret sin and began to feel a tug at his heart to go public with his testimony, he couldn't act on it right away. That was because someone very important in his life felt he should wait — his son, Shaun.

Still in high school, Shaun wanted to make it through those difficult teen years without ridicule and judgment and kindly asked his dad to wait until he was out of high school to break the news. It was no secret to Shaun, however, who said he was told at age 13 about his dad's homosexual lifestyle. But in a February 2009 interview, at age 22, Shaun admitted it took a long time for his young, innocent mind to even make sense of it all.

"I mean, I knew my dad was different than other dads in some way, but I didn't know how," he said.

Because of his dad's profession as a hairdresser, Shaun said people would often raise questions about his dad, asking him if his dad was gay. He would always answer, "No way."

Then, as he matured and learned more about what that word actually meant, things in his dad's life started to make sense. "Things started to click," he said.

***

Jonathan and his son have shared a unique bond from day one — a bond that would only grow stronger with time as a mature young man watched his dad rise up out of a shameful lifestyle and become mature himself in his walk with Christ.

Christopher Shaun Ervin was born on July 7, 1987. Jonathan has vivid memories of his birth.

> "They wrapped Shaun in a blanket and put him in my arms first, because they were still working on his mom. I was laughing with joy and crying at the same time. I had never known the power of a father's love until that moment. I never knew it was humanly possible to love that deeply. My heart could not contain the love and joy I felt in that amazing moment.
>
> "I totally forgot I had a camera with me, the world completely stopped as I held in my arms this amazing gift of God to us. The pediatrician quickly grabbed my camera and captured that first embrace.
>
> "It was one of the most incredible events in my 25 years. A beautiful, healthy, baby boy. Now I

was a dad, I couldn't believe it. I cannot begin to measure the boundless love that flooded my heart with this amazing gift of God to us. I was over-joyed with the power of a father's love. Without question, becoming a father was the most incred-ible experience and joy I have ever known."

Even after the divorce five years later, when Jonathan was deep into the homosexual lifestyle, ironically he knew his son needed to be pointed in the right direction. He wanted Shaun to grow up with a Christian influence and agreed with Shaun's mother to enroll Shaun at the private Liberty Christian Academy, a ministry of Thomas Road Baptist Church. It was through a program there that Shaun would come to know Christ.

Shaun Ervin shares many of his dad's characteristics; his wide smile, his creative mind and ... his musical talent.

"We sound exactly alike," Shaun said in a February 2009 interview at age 22. "If you're out of the room and hear one of us sing, you couldn't tell who it was. We sound the same."

Shaun has always sung in school chorus, performed in school plays and after high school graduation, he toured out West with a singing group called Living Proof.

He did a duet with his father on Father's Day at their church in 2005 — "Amazing Grace."

"Getting asked to do a duet with my son on Father's Day was the highlight of all my singing opportunities," Jonathan said.

Perhaps it was all those lullabies Jonathan sang him as a baby, even before he was born, that brought about Shaun's love for music as well.

"While Shaun was being wonderfully created in his mother's womb, I would often cup my hands on Ellen's stomach and sing to Shaun. After he was born, there were times when nothing would calm him down, then I would start singing that song to him that I did before he was born, and he would immediately just relax and calm down."

Shaun and his dad also share the same alma mater. Shaun was a freshman at Liberty University when his dad was invited to share his testimony and sing at one of the weekly convocations. In the basketball arena, with about 8,000 students in attendance, Jonathan's filmed interview was shown and he stood up to sing. He was introduced as a man living with AIDS. He was also introduced as the parent of a Liberty student.

"I was way up at the top. I kept praying, 'Please don't say my name; please don't say my name,'" Shaun recalls. "I heard him sing and then I left quickly with a friend."

He said it wasn't shame he was feeling then, but more of his shy nature coming through. Unlike his father, who has no trouble playing lead roles at the theater, Shaun is more withdrawn. He prefers casual, one-on-one conversation and said he is "more laid-back" than his dad.

"He runs headstrong into things," Shaun said, laughing as he recalled a time with his dad when he literally ran right into trouble.

"It was wintertime and it was night and my dad just had this idea we should go sleigh-riding. We went out to an open field and got on a sled together and went down a hill in the dark. We ended up in a briar patch; my dad had briars all over him."

The two have been on other thrill rides together. Jonathan was with Shaun on his first elephant ride at the circus, on his first helicopter flight, first hot air balloon flight, and on many a roller coaster, golf carts and jet skis.

When Shaun was in his care on weekends, Jonathan would plan special outings for them.

"One our favorite things to do was pack a picnic and drive up to the Peaks of Otter (part of the Blue Ridge mountains) and put down a big blanket and enjoy the view. When Shaun turned 5 years old, I promised him on that day I would take him to hike to the top. It was a great accomplishment for him."

And there were many fun vacations over the years — just the two of them.

"When Shaun was in middle school we took a special father/son trip to Las Vegas," Jonathan said. "We stayed at the Excalibur Hotel. This trip was fantastic. We did a 2.5-hour horseback ride through the Red Rock Canyons, took an Indian-guided tour of the Grand Canyon, saw Lake Mead and Hoover Dam. We were making memories together."

A few years after Jonathan found out he had HIV/AIDS, he took his then 16-year-old son to Cancun, Mexico for spring break.

"We both share an incredible love for the ocean. We stayed at a nice resort, parasailed together, snorkeled over the coral reef, and took a Jungle tour on a jet ski through the Gulf of Mexico into the Caribbean Sea."

But there is one memory the two wish they never had.

"It's always something I'll have with me — finding out my dad has AIDS," Shaun said.

Jonathan recalls the moment he broke the news to his son, then age 13.

"In all of this, the one most difficult area was how would I tell my sweet baby boy, as I love to call him, that I had AIDS? I was praying for God to show me the right time, and yet, how would there ever be a right time? I had lived a life in secret to protect Shaun and now I had to confess to my child that I had a terminal disease because of my choices.

"He was home with me for a weekend and we were sitting together in the living room. There was no way to make this easy for him or me. As parents, we spend our child's entire life trying to protect them from hurts and disappointments ... and now I had to share this part of my life with my son.

"I simply told Shaun that after my divorce I backslid away from God. And that sometime during those years, I had become infected with the HIV Virus and had AIDS. The mood was somber and very tense. My then 13- or 14-year-old son went back to his bedroom and laid on his bed. I followed him back there, crawled up on his bed with him and held him as he began to weep. It was the most heart-wrenching experience I've ever had in my life."

Jonathan wanted to prepare his son for everything. He started by quickly educating him on how the disease is transmitted, "to help alleviate any of Shaun's unknown fears that he could catch this from me," he said. He gathered up some documentaries that would help Shaun understand what a person with AIDS has to endure.

"They were awful, but they really helped me see what AIDS is about," Shaun said. And they also helped him see what a miracle God had done in his dad's life by keeping him healthy for so long.

"Those people in those movies were at the same stage in the disease as my dad and they were just skin and bones," Shaun said in 2009. "God's hand is definitely on my dad. There's no other way."

Jonathan said he also took hold of every opportunity to teach Shaun all the life lessons he wanted him to learn.

"I didn't know how long I would live before this disease would take me, so I began just sharing life lessons with Shaun every time we were together. I wanted him to learn from the mistake I had made."

Even though Shaun has learned some hard life lessons through his dad's bad decisions, he said since his dad's diagnosis, he has taught him to "never give up, no matter how hard a situation gets and to just keep my focus always on Christ, no matter what."

And if there's one thing Jonathan would have wanted his son to learn from life, that was it. If he had learned that earlier in his own life, he may not have made the choices he had that led him down those dark corridors of life when he was his son's age.

Shaun attended the service when his father first went public about his former gay lifestyle. In the congregation were people he had grown up with. He shared his dad's nervousness and anxiety at what would come of it all. No longer could he answer "No way" when people asked. He knew years before that his dad would eventually make this step of faith, but he admits he didn't want to be there when the time had finally come.

"With something like that, I was just on pins and needles the whole time," Shaun said after that night at Thomas Road Baptist Church. "But everything went according to God's plan and it worked out great. ... I really admire his bravery for what he is doing with his testimony. I really admire the stand for Christ that he is taking publicly. I don't think I could do it."

Every father hopes his son will call him his "hero" someday. Jonathan, although he hid a secret lifestyle from his son for many years, was no exception.

But that day did come. Just as Jonathan had made a simple gesture to his own father by sending a card a few years before, now it was his son's turn. Jonathan treasures this note, hand-written by Shaun, in a Father's Day card to him in 2008, seven months after he went public with his redemption story:

> Hey Dad,
>
> I just wanted to let you know how PROUD I am of everything you have accomplished this year! What a giant leap of faith you have taken in going public with your testimony! A true hero is willing to take risks in order to glorify the name of Christ ... you're my hero. I love and appreciate you more than you'll ever know!
>
> Happy Father's Day!!,
> Shaun

CHAPTER 9
Friends To The End

A t the toughest times in our lives, it helps us to know there are many strong arms holding us up, encouraging us to endure the struggles of life that come and go like the ocean tides — all the way until the day we take our final breath.

Jonathan's family continued to support him and love him after he went public with his testimony of a changed life, but there are a few friends who have been with him through much of his hardship and those friends will be with him to the end. Looking back, Jonathan believes God has placed certain people in his life for this purpose. And he is more grateful than ever for their friendship as he faces his final days on earth.

***

For all of his adult life, Jonathan has lived at least a 12-hour drive away from his family. Having someone with whom he could share his daily struggles was always important to him, especially after his divorce. That's when Sandy Bradshaw came into his life.

"Unlike most men who can't share their feelings verbally, I can. I have always been in touch with my true feelings and have to verbalize them and Sandy has been that person I have done that with.

"Sandy would listen to me and let me express my hurts, frustrations, etc. and would just love me unconditionally. She never judged me or turned her ear away, she just loved me right where I was at. Little did I know many years later why God had brought this very special lady into my life."

Sandy started out as a mere acquaintance, the mother of a friend Jonathan worked with at a hair salon who would stop by and see her daughter occasionally. They would invite Jonathan to have coffee or lunch with them and Jonathan enjoyed the company. Sandy and Jonathan quickly hit it off and their relationship grew to be more like family.

"After several months I asked Sandy if she would be my 'adopted Lynchburg mom' because I didn't have family here. That day a friendship was forged unlike any I had ever had. She was the same age as my mom and a widow. I called her "Mom," and she would call me her son. We would spend time together, movies, dinner, etc. I think she is probably one of the funniest people I've ever met in my life. We just had so much fun together and this was filling a void in my life not having my mom close by."

It also helped Sandy, because she admits she was going through empty nest syndrome after her daughter moved out and got married. "Jonathan and I have been very close friends," she said. "I talk to him almost daily — he calls me early in the morning and we have coffee together on the phone."

What Jonathan didn't know when he first met Sandy was how *much* he would need her — especially when he would learn he was dying of AIDS.

"The amazing thing about all this," Sandy said, "is I'm a hospice nurse."

Sandy has been a nurse for 40 years. It's no consequence that she would become Jonathan's closest friend.

"I have to think this whole meeting [with Jonathan] was by God's design because God knew even before I met Jonathan what his future held," she said. "Because of my experience and my love for Jonathan, I told him I would be with him ... until the end."

If there was anyone who was not surprised when they heard the news he had HIV, it was Sandy. She knew the lifestyle he had been leading because the two of them had gotten close enough for her to confront him about it — as a friend.

"I suspected when I first met Jonathan that he was leading this lifestyle — just too many things did not add up. I asked him bluntly and he said, 'Yes I am.' I told him: 'I want you to know that it's not going to make any difference to me in how I feel about you; if anything, I don't condone that lifestyle, but if you need someone to talk to, you can talk to me.'"

Sandy admits her views about homosexuality did not match Jonathan's at the time, but she believed her role first and foremost was to love him — and pray.

"After he told me he was gay, I knew that he continued with that lifestyle but from that point I have loved him unconditionally and accepted him where he was. I never preached at him — I prayed for him a lot — but I never preached at him. One sin is no greater than another."

In April 2000, after receiving a phone call from his doctor informing him he had tested positive for HIV, the first person he told was his "adopted Lynchburg mom." They quickly made plans to make a memory together and took a cruise to the southern Caribbean Sea. Back at home, he shared with her every three months his lab work showing the virus destroying his immune system. Though sad to see the count drop, she was happy when, five years later, she was the first one to see the renovation begin in Jonathan's heart. No one could have been happier to see him make this turnaround, knowing all the more where he was coming from. She was a proud mom.

"He called me one night and said 'Mama I think the Lord is calling me to go public with this' —I said, 'Jonathan, are you sure?' because he had worked hard all his life to keep it from everybody. He said, 'Yes, if it can help somebody.' When he made the appointment with Jonathan Falwell, I knew he was sincere. I can honestly say since that time I have never suspected that he has stepped back into that lifestyle — he has been on the straight and narrow, he really has. He's not just talking the talk; Jonathan is truly living his life to honor God first."

But Sandy knows her role is far from over. She still must see her friend through the most difficult time in his life. She remembers a time, before Jonathan was diagnosed with AIDS, when he asked her how the disease affects people. She told him about the terrible opportunistic infections that AIDS patients can contract that end up ultimately killing them, and she described the suffering many have to endure.

"He said, 'Really? All that can happen?' I said, 'All that and more.' I said AIDS can make cancer look like a picnic and it's true." She said that conversation rings in her head sometimes. "I wish I'd never said that to him, but maybe subconsciously I thought it might influence some of his choices. Taking care of AIDS patients is "heart-wrenching," she said, "but for one thing, I have been a nurse since 1963 so over the years I have really learned to accept people where they are. I don't believe I've ever been judgmental, just supportive and making them as comfortable as I can."

Jonathan knows he will have to endure much and he has prepared — far more than any patient Sandy can recall.

"I've never had a hospice patient even who has prepared as much for their death as he has."

She knew he had purchased a grave marker and had it installed. She helped him write his funeral plans.

Sandy said even though she has seen many patients die, she's probably less prepared for death than her friend.

"I never get used to death, I really don't," she said. "It's nothing for me to cry with the family, cry with the patient. There are patients I can be real close to and having known him for 15 years, now helping him plan his funeral, it's really hard."

But she said she feels some peace nonetheless.

"That is not to say that I will not be upset and miss him terribly, but when God is finished with Jonathan on this earth — I truly believe he's leaving him here to share with more people and bring them to Christ — when he's finished with his work here, I'm OK to let him go."

Sandy was there, of course, when Jonathan first shared his testimony that night at Thomas Road Baptist Church in November 2007. And there were two other friends close by that wouldn't have missed it for the world. Though they spent most of their adult life many, many miles apart, these two friends shared a special bond with Jonathan — one that started during their college days.

Curt Motsinger, a seminary student and former senior pastor from Rose City, Mich., and David Barstead, a produce/retail store owner in Ontario, Canada, met Jonny at Liberty Baptist College when they were all freshmen. Curt remembers hearing this slow southern drawl in front of him at the registration line.

"I don't know that I had ever met such a southern boy as him. ... He was with a bunch of his friends from Memphis, Tenn., and he did everything so slow ... and he talked sooooo slow. I couldn't help it... I was just laughing and finally he just turned around and said 'What?' I told him he was just funny, and he tried to be stern but then just made a silly face and cracked up."

The two ended up being in the same dorm, where they both met David and all three were close friends for the next two years, eating meals together, going out on triple dates together and even sneaking around together. One time they got themselves in big trouble when they snuck off campus to a hotel and went swimming. Curt recalls the incident.

"We fell asleep and had to sneak back on campus (after curfew). We saw this security truck pull up next to us and

Jonny's going, 'Let's run.' And I said, 'No we're just gonna make it worse if we run.' So we got in the truck and the one guy got on a walkie-talkie and said, 'We've apprehended the suspects.' Jonny and I just looked at each other and we both made that same silly face he did when we met."

He said whenever he was with Jonny, he could count on laughs. "He's got such a quick wit about him."

One time as they were walking through a crowded area of campus, Jonathan broke into song (which wasn't uncommon for him), Curt said. But the song he sang off the top of his head was a secular hit at the time and listening to anything but Christian music was frowned upon at the conservative Baptist college.

"From the top of his lungs, with that big ole voice, he started singing, 'I've been waiting ... .' Heads just jerked and looked at him. (The rest of the verse goes, 'for a girl like you to come into my life ...') and then it him that it was a secular song, but he didn't miss a beat, he just sang, "for the Lord to come ..." (in the same tune). It was hysterical. We just had so much fun with Jonny; he's got this zest for life."

But that zest for life would soon lead him to leave his friends behind to pursue their degrees as he tried a stint in New York City, hoping to make it into show business.

"When Jonny left, I was surprised, but not really surprised," David said. "I knew he had just had so much ambition musically. He wanted to take it to the next level and I always thought he would; I always expected to see Jonny travelling somewhere with some group or doing something big with it."

Curt said it was hard for him to support his decision.

"When he went to go to New York City, I kind of gave him the what-for — and then I was afraid that he was just running and he was after world success and not God's success. When he went, he distanced himself from things he actually loved."

But despite their differences of opinion, Jonathan still stayed in close contact with his friends, even after they had graduated and returned home to pursue their own careers and raise their families. Jonathan would always make sure he had a current phone number to call his friends — even if it was just once a year.

"Sure enough the phone would ring on my birthday and it would be Jonny," David said.

Jonathan had a way of remembering his friends' birthdays: Curt's was the same as his dad's and David's was the same as his mom's. Sometimes, he would call his friends on the holidays.

"Jonny is responsible for that (keeping in touch over the years); he's the one who's reached out the most, to keep the friendships alive," Curt said.

But when they both got that unexpected phone call from Jonathan telling them he had AIDS and had been living a homosexual lifestyle, it was more important than any other call they had received from him for the past 20 years.

The old friends were shocked and saddened by the news.

"It definitely was a secret place because I never suspected it," David said. "I had no idea; here we were best friends and it never even dawned on me or crossed my mind."

Curt said there was always "a suspicion but never anything to confirm it ... because we did talk about girls and all of that when we were in college."

But swallowing the news that their friend had AIDS drew out the strongest emotions.

"We cried and then laughed," Curt said. "But it didn't affect our friendship at all, in fact it probably deepened it. You realize that our love for each other was unconditional."

So much so that Curt wanted Jonathan to move to Michigan.

"I was concerned he would die alone. I wanted him to come here, live with us and help us start a ministry in this area, but obviously he wanted to stay close to Shaun," Curt said.

So when Jonathan invited both of his friends to fly to Lynchburg to support him when he shared his testimony for the first time, they both said they would drop everything and come.

And that wasn't easy for David, who owned his own business and spent any free time he had with his wife and four kids. He had not seen Jonny or been back to Lynchburg in more than 20 years.

"When he called and said, 'I need you guys to come down,' I said, 'Uh-oh this is serious,'" David said. "It was a last-minute thing, but I had to be there — there was no question. Whatever it took I would go, I'd fill in the holes when I got back. I'm sure glad I went. It certainly wasn't a mistake."

Jonathan was excited for the reunion. He met them both at the airport, where his amazingly healthy persona surprised them both.

"We were expecting to see him not looking so well," David said. "I was surprised. We went out to eat and had a great time — it was just like the old Jonny. It was just like we hadn't left; the friendship was still strong. It was unbelievable ... I hadn't seen these guys for so long, but yet we picked up like we had just talked last week."

They spent the brief weekend reminiscing, looking at old pictures and even touring the campus, where they were surprised to see their old dorm still standing amidst all the new buildings that had sprouted up since they left.

But seeing Jonathan give his testimony — and seeing what happened immediately afterward — was definitely the highlight.

CHAPTER 10
A Sea Of Support

Ann Saunders remembers it was a "bit of a cry fest" the night Jonathan told her and his other coworkers at the salon that he had AIDS.

"It was very sad, and it was unexpected. It's one thing when he tells you 'I have AIDS,' but in the same breath 'I've got six months to live' — that was a little hard to digest and still is," she said in February 2009.

Emily Casper Brown, who owned the salon along with Saunders, said she respected the fact Jonathan came to them and told them in person. And when Jonathan invited the staff to come see his testimony that Sunday night in November 2007, she said they wouldn't have missed it; they even rounded up some family members to come along.

Jonathan was looking forward to seeing his friends, even some of those clients, there that night, but when it came time for the service to close, they were all hard to find — not because they weren't there, but because they were mingled in with a large crowd of people waiting their turn to speak with Jonathan Ervin.

***

At the end of that service, after Pastor Jonathan Falwell had called Jonathan back on stage and after everyone bowed their heads to pray for him, Jonathan turned to Falwell.

"The service was over and I'm up there thanking him [Falwell] for the opportunity and he said, 'You don't need to talk to me right now, there's a lot of people that want to speak to you.' So I looked down and there was a sea of people, all the way to the back of the church."

Pastor Falwell remembers that special moment.

"He had a circle of people that went out 15-20 feet around him — ALL the way around — that were waiting to talk with him, and loving him and praying with him. It over-whelmed him — and it overwhelmed me because it showed this is a healthy church, because that's what churches are supposed to do."

Jonathan was there for over an hour, shaking hands and receiving hugs from old friends, new friends and people he didn't even know. Curt Motsinger said he was relieved to see so much support for his friend. He had worried, being so far away in Michigan, that that wouldn't happen.

"Jonathan is such a friend to so many people, I was just afraid ... there's this guy who's loved by so many people, I was just afraid that the Christians would be the ones who would not be there with him ... and friendship means so much to him. But that night, I saw he has a church family."

Jonathan said he certainly felt their compassion, but is also quick to say he did not seek their sympathy.

"It's not that I wanted sympathy, but what I was hoping was that this would open doors for a lot of people ... because there are many who struggle in the Secret Place, to know that they do have a choice. And I'm telling my story because I wanted to inspire other people to live a committed life to Christ all the way through."

It was a huge outpouring in his church, he said, "And it's been that way anywhere I've shared it or told it. That's God's blessing. It could have gone either way."

At Thomas Road Baptist Church, the reaction was over-whelming, Jonathan said, but after hearing a story a few weeks later, he knows it was also just another way God had answered the prayer of a faithful servant who was now living with God in glory.

"A client of mine, whose father-in-law, Charlie Judd, was there that night when I first gave my testimony, told me this story. She said Charlie, who was involved with the Moral Majority with Dr. Jerry Falwell, Sr., was called into a private meeting with Falwell over 20 years ago. When they went behind closed doors, Falwell said, 'There are two people I believe who are involved in homosexuality and I want us to lift them up in prayer.' I was one of the names."

After being told that story, Jonathan went to bed that night and had a dream about the late Dr. Jerry Falwell.

"In the dream he said nothing, but had this huge smile on his face looking at me, giving me the thumbs-up while shaking his fist," Jonathan recalls. "It was as if he was so happy about what God has done in my life and was encouraging me in the faith. ... I could not help but rejoice knowing that Dr. Falwell has watched from heaven — his prayer having been answered that was lifted so many years ago on my behalf."

Jonathan has felt that encouragement from many others.

"I've gotten nothing but [compassion] from church members, from co-workers, from clientele ... there's been not one negative outburst. That was the biggest thing I was afraid of, you know, that I'd lose my job, then my home, my car ... none of that has happened, and I think that's God's blessing for obedience. My business is even busier. There are people on a waiting list still trying to get in," he said in February 2009.

But the real blessing is the family of God — his own glimpse of heaven here on earth.

"The great thing that has come out about this is showing that the church doesn't need to stand in judgment of other people because of a lifestyle, because it's a sin just like any other sin. We're born into a sin nature: yours may be drugs, alcohol, pornography, whatever.

"I think it's a great thing that we're talking about this now. Because there are many people out there hiding, they have fallen into a sin or a lifestyle, it's secret, and they need to know the church is here for them, to support them, to live a committed Christian life."

EPILOGUE

F acing the end of your life, death can be a very unsettling thing. You seem to take into account all the many events of your life. As I have done that, I see God's mighty hand woven like a tapestry all throughout my now 47 years.

As I am writing this book, I have only 19 T cells remaining in my immune system. There is no doubt God has literally sustained my health to accomplish what He has called me to do. I can actually say that AIDS has become one of the greatest blessings in my life. Because of this disease, I have been brought into a relationship with God that I have only read about in a book.

Now, looking at the end of my life ... it doesn't feel like the end, but rather the beginning. It's as if this life has been one big classroom and every experience, good or bad, has been a teaching and growing experience. Of all the many lessons learned in this journey of life, the greatest for me has been how to forgive.

It certainly was the most difficult lesson to learn, but with God's help He taught me how. To forgive ... wow, it completely frees your spirit like a bird taking flight.

The Bible teaches that what Satan means for evil, God means for good ... and that all things work together for good to those who are called according to His purpose. (Romans 8:28)

Just remember when you were a child and your family was planning a special trip. The excitement and anticipation would build as you got closer and closer to that trip. That is how I feel inside as I look toward heaven. I cannot wait to get there. I can't wait to climb up into God's lap like a little boy and feel His loving arms around me. Finally I will feel His comfort, love, and protection from all harm.

God loves you and created you for his pleasure. From the beginning of time in the Garden of Eden, it was never God's intention that man suffer any sickness, pain, or even a physical death. He didn't create us as robots, but rather gave us free will. With the fall of Adam and Eve into sin, it started a ball in motion. God declared that the wages of sin would be death, but the gift of God is eternal life through Jesus Christ our Lord. (Romans 6:23)

It doesn't matter about your religious faith or upbringing. Jesus said in John chapter 14, "I am the way and the truth and the life. No one comes to the Father except through me." God is a loving and forgiving God, but he is also very holy and right-eous. He could not allow sinners into heaven. And that is what the crucifixion was all about. God made a special provision for our forgiveness of sins. It is offered to all of mankind as a free gift ... eternal life. But it is ultimately your choice.

It is my deepest desire that this book will inspire all who read it, and that they would seek a personal relationship with God through his son, Jesus Christ, and for all believers, that they will be encouraged to stay committed to Christ ... all the way to the finish line.

Until we meet again ...

Completely His,

Jonathan Ervin

ABOUT THE AUTHORS

F*or updates and contact information, visit:*

www.JonathanErvin.com

As long as God sustains his health, Jonathan will welcome the opportunity to share his story with your church or organization.

Mitzi Bible lives with her husband, Jimmy, and their two children, Lydia and Jarod, in Lynchburg, Va. She began her communications career in Christian television and has produced religion, news, lifestyle and community sections for newspapers in Texas and Virginia. She is a freelance writer for home and lifestyle magazines in Virginia and a full-time writer and editor with the University Advancement office at Liberty University.

Contact her at mobible@liberty.edu.